Lead Generation

Lead Generation and Marketing Strategies for Start-up

(Create a Marketing System That Will Win New Business Clients for Your High Value Service)

Kevin Mettler

Published By **Ryan Princeton**

Kevin Mettler

Lead Generation: Lead Generation and Marketing Strategies for Start-up (Create a Marketing System That Will Win New Business Clients for Your High Value Service)

ISBN   978-1-998769-84-1

Legal & Disclaimer

from and against any damages, costs, and expenses, including any legal fees potentially resulting from the application of any of the information provided by this guide. This disclaimer applies to any damages or injury caused by the use and application, whether directly or indirectly, of any advice or information presented, whether for breach of contract, tort, negligence, personal injury, criminal intent, or under any other cause of action.

You agree to accept all risks of using the information presented inside this book. You need to consult a professional medical practitioner in order to ensure you are both able and healthy enough to participate in this program.

Table Of Contents

Chapter 1: The Concept Of Lead Generation

What is a Lead?

A lead is any character who indicates interest in a enterprise's service or product in some manner, shape, or form. Leads usually listen from a enterprise or business enterprise after starting communication (with the aid of filing non-public information for an offer, trial, or subscription) … as an alternative of having a random cold name from someone who purchased their contact statistics.

Let's say you take a web survey to study more about how to take care of your automobile. A day or so later, you get hold of an electronic mail from the car organisation that created the survey approximately how they could help you cope with your car. This system would be some distance much less intrusive than in the event that they'd just called you suddenly with out a information of whether you even care about car

1

maintenance, right? This is what it's like to be a lead.

And from a commercial enterprise attitude, the records the auto organization collects about you out of your survey responses enables them personalize that beginning verbal exchange to address your existing troubles - and not waste time calling leads who aren't at all inquisitive about auto services.

Leads are part of the wider lifecycle that customers comply with once they transition from tourist to patron. Not all leads are created equal, nor are they qualified the identical.

There are unique kinds of leads primarily based on how they're certified and what lifecycle level they're in:

- Marketing Qualified Lead

- Sales Qualified Lead

- Product Qualified Lead

- Service Qualified Lead

What is Lead Generation?

Lead generation is the system of attracting and converting strangers and possibilities into someone who has indicated an interest to your enterprise's service or product. Some examples of lead mills are task applications, weblog posts, coupons, live activities, and online content. These lead generators are only some examples of lead era strategies you could use to draw potential customers and manual them in the direction of your gives. (We will speak about more techniques later).

Whenever someone outdoor the advertising world asks me what I do, I can't sincerely say, "I create content for lead generation." It'd be completely misplaced on them, and I'd get some without a doubt confused seems. So alternatively, I say, "I work on finding particular approaches to draw human beings to my enterprise. I need to offer them with sufficient sweets to get them naturally interested by my employer, so that they sooner or later heat up to the brand sufficient to need to listen from us!"

That commonly resonates better, and that's exactly what lead generation is: It's a way of warming up potential clients on your business and getting them on the path to finally making a purchase.

Lead technology describes the advertising method of stimulating and shooting hobby in a products or services for the reason of developing a sales pipeline. Lead era frequently uses digital channels and has been present process substantial adjustments in current years from the rise of recent online and social techniques. In unique, the abundance of facts quite simply to be had on line has led to the rise of the "self-directed customer" and the emergence of recent strategies to develop and qualify capacity leads earlier than passing them to income.

Chapter 2: The Importance Of Lead Generation For Small And Medium-Sized Enterprises (Sme)

Traditionally, lead generation is finished by way of attending conferences, trade suggests, fairs, and other public activities, where the company showcases its products or services to attendees. These traditional styles of lead generation may be an effective shape of generating sales but can also be an expense that companies have to shoulder. For SMEs, this can critically put a dent in their coins float. Although cash is allocated for such campaigns, companies have to add more resources to ensure sales.

Online Lead Generation

As society today is bombarded with an abundance of information through the web, prospective customers have the ability to advantage greater information approximately the product(s) they're inquisitive about and can delay talking with different companies to know the products or services they offer. This leads to the demise of print advertising, trade indicates, and bloodless calling, as they have become inappropriate. To combat these phenomena, online lead generation was born. This lead type is the latest marketing tool that big companies employ to cut their marketing expenses with out limiting their ability to benefit new leads.

Types of Online Lead Generation

There are several methods to generate leads on the internet, which are accessible and free for many companies. One of the famous approaches of doing this is through online surveys. Online surveys provide the enterprise a basic overview of their target marketplace's reviews, preferences as well as interests. By carrying out a survey, organizations can tailor-fit their product(s) to match the public's interest.

Paid Advertising

For companies that have a few budget, they may opt for pay-per-click lead generation. This is a advertising and marketing tool that will rate the company for each click that it receives, and the cost might rely on the company's finances. Pay consistent with click is not for everyone. Granted, value per click may seem small at the onset, however it can be high-priced together. It can lead some prospective customers to the site, but a sale is not guaranteed and charges may be some distance more than what it's far budgeted for.

Organic Reach

Another way to generate sales leads is through organic reach, e. G. Key-word search consequences. Many websites offer free lead era based totally on the keywords the company aims to recognize. As lead results obtained from such practices are often the result of organic search or searches done by interested individuals, the potential to close a sale is extraordinarily likely compared to traditional marketing activities. This advertising tool is essential to the success of SME enterprises as it objectives the market they are interested in, especially if they are concerned or want to target certain locations where they can offer their services.

five Reasons Why You Need Lead Generation for Your Business

Before we study the strategies, on this bankruptcy you'll discover a top level view of the primary reasons and advantages of lead generation:

1. Easy Customer Interaction

Staying close to your clients is one great way you may be assured of a good customer-business relationship. You need to interact properly with your clients, proportion thoughts and a whole lot more about the offerings you offer and how it benefits your customers. Leads enable you to pitch your product to customers each time they request information from your business. When you create a solid customer interaction mechanism, you stand a better chance of building a trustworthy and long-lasting relationship with your customers.

2. High Conversion Rates

Lead generation often outcomes in a higher conversion rate when compared with other cold contact strategies. This is due to the fact lead possibilities are often pre-qualified, even earlier than you get the lead. As a business, you don't should worry about how to generate leads for your products or services. What is critical is that you are capable of converting your site visitors into potential customers.

3. Lead Generation is a Great Tool for Growing Your Business

Lead era is critical for business growth. With a nicely-idea-out lead generation strategy, you can increase sales with the aid of using traffic to your website. You can also get a higher conversion rate, which basically effects in a higher income margin.

four. Leads Can Be Controlled to Target Specific Areas

You can never serve everyone in the global with your products or offerings. However, this does not mean that you should start limiting your self to serve simplest a few clients. Using leads allows you to customize the geographical location of your target clients or where you are involved in. This way that you need to do good research on where your real customers are.

five. You Can Share Leads With Businesses in the Same Niche

No business can operate in isolation, and that may be a reality. We need every other, even if we are competition. Understanding how other businesses are doing can be a great motivation on your part. Lead generation is good, as you can without difficulty share leads with businesses inside the identical niche. It works perfectly nicely, especially for businesses that promote complementary items.

Lead generation is a great tool that every business owner must embrace. Its benefits cannot be overemphasized as they truely stand out.

The Value of a Lead Generation Service

Lead generation is becoming one in all the most effective internet marketing techniques for almost any type of business. The vast majority of online entrepreneurs are using this method to gain more and more potential customers on the internet every day. Lead generation involves the generation of consumer interest in products or services. In addition to making sales, this method can be used to provide e-newsletters as well as list building.

In order to understand how the technique works, it is important to understand what you should remember when applying this commercial enterprise merchandising method. The most important factor to consider is the quality of your leads. You honestly need to focus on producing qualified leads. These are those who are particularly looking for products and services that you are offering.

As you discovered in bankruptcy 2, certified leads can be acquired through paid advertising or organic attain. When people search for specific information on the internet, chances are that they will land proper on your webpage. This method isn't like the usual traditional paperwork of advertising like radio, print media or tv adverts that involve approaching people randomly.

One of the major reasons why you should use a lead generation service to promote your business is that the internet has become commonplace for a big number of potential clients. This means that enterprise proprietors should take this opportunity to meet more clients. However, the increase in eCommerce websites has brought about an increase in competition. This calls for specific and effective advertising techniques. A terrific manner to locate and keep potential clients is via lead generation.

A reliable lead generation carrier will not only ensure that you gain a big number of repeat clients, however you will be capable of maintain them as properly.

Even although your business establishment may sometimes be closed, people can still get facts about your business online. This is due to the fact the internet runs 24/7. Nowadays, you need to apply the fine techniques to maintain your business ahead of the competition. A desirable lead generation system will assist you respond to the leads before other groups seize them.

If you wish to get the best from lead generation, you may want to don't forget hiring a lead generation service. Generating leads requires skills and knowledge. Moreover, this method of enterprise promotion won't be powerful if you do not have access to the proper tools and resources. Furthermore, you have to understand that the complete process of generating leads can be time-consuming and complex, specially for beginners. You can keep all the time and effort by hiring a business enterprise that specializes in such services. Since there are many methods used to generate leads, a reliable organization will pick out the most powerful method to ensure you get qualified leads within a shorter period of time.

Hiring the services of a dependable lead generation online agency can help you perceive your targeted audience. Once you identify your target market, you must be quick to respond to their inquiries. Your leads should easily be converted to regular customers if nicely attended to.

Is Your Lead Generation Process Rewarding?

Without leads, no business, online or offline, can be a success. So understanding how to acquire highly targeted leads is going to be the powerhouse behind your worthwhile business. You might assume a lead is a lead, but you're wrong. Making a cold lead and a highly focused lead finally charges the same, but the latter is definitely much better. For instance, if leads haven't been qualified in the promotion process, then you may find yourself losing your time on unqualified and disinterested prospects. Your income reaction figures will drop, and business declines. It's a vicious cycle.

Is Your Lead Generation Process Time-Consuming?

Creating leads can be a labor-intensive method. An offline lead technology process means meeting prospects face to face in physical places as well as contacting them via smartphone. The leads that are generated at trade suggests and different events need to be placed in a database and made contact with one by one. Your business may need to mail information to the prospects, which can also be a luxurious pastime. Such leads must be qualified and then passed off to the firm's sales office, where a sale will perhaps be made inside the future. Online lead generation is much easier. But if you're the owner of your own network advertising company or internet promotion employer, you know that is not simply so. Rather than fishing in a sea searching for the right fish, you are fishing in an enormous ocean of people, none of whom have heard of you or your business!

Any business takes money and time to get it off the ground. The more money you can invest in your business, the more you can spend on hiring folk to do the time-intensive jobs or the things you just can't do. You can also spend money on advertising, which should bring in more leads. If an individual has made an appealing website, and he or she is following the tried and tested techniques of fulfillment, for example, making an investment in an auto-responder, rapidly answering mails, adding articles on a regular foundation, prominently displaying an opt-in box, building back-links and becoming a member of social media networks, he or she should be making cash. If not, it's time to restore it!

Should You Consider Outsourcing the Lead Generation Process?

As a business owner, you is probably thinking about outsourcing your lead technology procedure. And in case you are a bit skeptical about this, here you'll locate a few benefits of incorporating it into your commercial enterprise:

Having a company generate leads can prevent money compared to setting up advertising campaigns. You can imagine all the hustle and bustle involved in hiring middlemen, paying them their commissions and a good deal extra. With lead generation, you can be assured of slashed costs on lead acquisitions.

Buying qualified leads is pretty simple, in particular when you have decent abilities in it. Outsourcing this type of service saves you the time spent on servicing customers, because the provider company spends time attracting leads. It can save you a lot of the time you may have wasted using other methods.

Moreover, you only pay for the leads you have obtained. This means that you can save a substantial amount of cash with it.

You can also control the number of leads you want to receive monthly, hence budgeting can be very simple. Again, you will in no way waste your resources, as you could easily choose services or products you need to present to your prospects.

Chapter 3: Eight Lead Generation Strategies To Grow Your Business

Lead generation has turn out to be a necessity for groups to survive in the modern enterprise environment. It plays a very significant position in improving sales, especially on the subject of internet advertising and marketing. With developing opposition, it is very critical for a agency to develop lead generation strategies through the internet. Thus, what are the best ways to collect the names and contact details of prospective customers who are interested in learning greater about what your business has to offer?

In this chapter, we are able to discuss the top lead generation strategies you can adopt to maximize your profits and sales. This list does not encompass hiring specialized companies. But if you like to try things out first on your own, then this list will be beneficial:

1. Offer Free Services

Such as email newsletters, loose consultation, complimentary trials of your products or services and so on. It is a fact that people are extra attracted to banners or ads that contain the word "free". This is an effective mean of getting the details of clients who can also be interested in your products. Make sure that your newsletter is information-packed, well-timed, and full of hyperlinks to different assets.

2. Provide Webinars

Webinars are an excellent way to connect with humans who are genuinely interested in your products. You will be able to acquire contact information, purchase necessities, and other details about your prospective clients after they sign up for the webinar.

3. Include a Lead Generation Form on Your Website

Your company website is one of the most important tools you can use. When a customer visits your site, he or she will be prompted to enter his or her details in the online form. Also, include a toll-free customer care wide variety for inquiries and encourage your customers to call you.

4. Referral Programs

Referral programs for cutting-edge customers using your services are additionally an exceptional way of generating quality leads. Free gifts or bonuses may be offered for every successful referral.

5. Email Marketing

Email advertising remains one of few online marketing channels that has stood the check of time, even dealing with to live at the top of many enterprise-to-business (B2B) advertising lead generation approach alternatives.

The secret to its persistence is how e-mail marketing lends itself to driving technological innovations. For example, one in all the most important developments in electronic mail advertising and marketing for the time being, one which has generated superb effects for lots B2B agencies, is advertising automation. Put actually, advertising automation gear are approximately hybrid electronic mail marketing gear that connect to your customer relationship management (CRM) device to enable you to mechanically send relatively centered, personalised emails to leads.

What the new approaches of doing e-mail advertising approach is that even as conventional newsletters and e mail advertising and marketing are nonetheless critical, the ability to seize extra statistics on customers and use behavioral triggers has enabled B2B entrepreneurs to get lots smarter with how they target customers inside the inbox.

three Tips For Effective Email Marketing Campaigns

Email advertising is all approximately based communique and organising a relationship with customers. Here are a few hints to control e mail advertising and marketing successfully:

a) Personalization

Do now not treat each person generically. Personalized technique will get you closer your income goal in case you put your mind to constructing a robust relationship from the begin, which is what you want to establish in the course of your emails. Once a capability client can see that they are valued and visible as greater than simply quite a number, they're far more likely to concentrate and take note of what you have to mention. Stick to presenting an email with a purpose, so one can assist, inform and captivate.

b) Timing and persistance

If you're emailing to clients or leads in different time zones, thoughts your timing and stay continual. Your electronic mail timing is essential as is your persistence and patience. Not all people is going to turn out to be a guaranteed lead from one, two or 3 emails. You have to hold at it and hold presenting variable content material and records till you sooner or later be successful and make that leap forward. Do no longer shun bloodless email outright.

Cold emailing stays a fruitful manner to offer facts to people in a mass scale and in a professionally-constructed way. This publicity gateway holds strong ability as long as you layout a marketing campaign that goes hand-in-hand with your enterprise targets.

c) Continous testing and optimization

Experiment with concern lines, content inclusions, copy period, among others. It is usually a undertaking to get the proper cadence structure and content for an e-mail campaign. To deliver your email marketing campaign the danger it desires, you need to combine the diverse elements and see which of them are giving you the desired consequences. Always highlight the fee you provide. This have to usually outline your electronic mail content, and maintain the facts as virtually as viable especially while you're coping with the high-quality-qualified lead profiles.

6. Social Marketing

Social media gives you an remarkable possibility to apply some of well-known systems to launch significant lead era campaigns. LinkedIn, Facebook, Twitter, Instagram and Quora are all over the region and beckon with a purpose to make the most out of them. The organizations that apprehend the power of social media in generating each interest and real sales use it to generate and nurture hundreds of thousands of bucks worth of leads. Their experiences inform us the first-rate manner to approach those channels. But there are other methods to enhance lead and advertising and marketing excellent, that may similarly improve the way you manage campaigns. Of route, now not all channels will be flawlessly suitable to your enterprise and niche, so it's far essential to divide a while funding to each one hence.

three Tips for Generating Leads With Social Media

Understanding the character of every social network is vital, most customarily generated by using real discipline experience and personal use. Three matters stand out whilst you're coping with social media on your lead technology activities:

a) The virtue of experimentation

Social media can be unwieldy as your weather proverbs and it being a relatively nascent discipline for even the savviest sales and advertising specialists, you want to get your hands grimy and do the actual works via going via trial and error levels to peer which method produces the favored outcomes.

b) Play with content material variant

Create a database of ideas and try them out for checking out and outcomes tracking. Be regular. Commit to consistent pastime and continuously engage together with your target audience.

c) Automate

Automating posting of content on social media can without difficulty be treated with the aid of many structures nowadays, so attempt to automate as much as possible. This will save you time and let you maximize your productivity to recognition on opportunity lead technology routes.

7. Content Marketing

Content marketing truely factors to the ones articles on your website, e-newsletters, weblog articles, video materials, or those substances which you submit for your social media channels to have interaction your leads, generate hobby and bring real income. Though content material advertising is regularly related to enterprise-to-patron (B2C), content material advertising can be effortlessly transitioned to the B2B industry with shift in technique, basically following the equal intentions but adapting the concepts to the needs of the B2B industry and the humans in it.

B2B content advertising is first-class aligned with your search engine optimization (search engine marketing) strategy, with the give up view of dominating search engine results so that it will vicinity your self in which your ability clients are searching.

Content advertising and marketing is king inside the virtual age - the best inbound solution. Its effect won't be as direct as a physical save, however its impact surely performs out longer than you can imagine whilst producing amazing outcomes. Not simplest will prospects discover you with absolute ease, however they will additionally come to believe your advice as you advantage authority and begin that each one-important client-purchaser courting manner. To make an effective content, you shouldn't lose sight of why you are generating content material within the first region, that's to generate actual paying clients.

How Content Relates to the Sales Funnel

In phrases of the income funnel version, you're going to manual your content material the identical manner you need to guide your content clients: down the trails of top of the funnel, center of the funnel, right down to the lowest of the funnel.

a) Top of the funnel content material

This is content material designed round large subjects, your foothold to visibility and gaining consciousness of your business and emblem. These should entail attachment to articles, infographics, even movies all showcasing the framework of your logo identity. This extensive place net approach will give you the best variety of visitors however the lowest direct conversions. This unfiltered section takes in such extent of humans although a lot of whom are far away from producing your ideal consumer profile. Outside of this immediate funnel issue, you need to keep in mind time and resources put into this style of content material effect your branded seek terms, build your area authority and provide you with electronic mail subscribers and a social media following - all of which contribute to the overall funnel and for retargeting parameters, a manner to disregard and qualify information approximately the target market you need to be using towards.

b) Middle of the funnel content

The 2nd degree of your content material marketing plan have to attention in your enterprise mainly. The center funnel is a place to present away recommendation and recommendations to end up the hub for valid enterprise information.

c) Bottom of the funnel content

At this point, customers are well-informed and best a quick distance away from the decision to shop for. They simplest want a few small decision-making aids to make a buy. To supply the very last impetus, success tales and wonderful feedback from different clients may be played out, as an instance. Discount offers which can be handiest valid for a certain time period can also offer the important incentive.

If your recommendation is depended on, then your product and provider will observe. A nicely-applied industry funnel ought to push you as a proper notion chief among the decision-makers to your industry. This may be extraordinarily powerful: a nice weblog or publication releasing common content material this is in call for offers your business a big possibility to develop with effective publicity levels.

8. Word-of-Mouth Marketing

The last and perhaps, the most important and effective strategy is word-of-mouth marketing. Good vintage word-of-mouth via social media sites, chat web sites, blog remarks, and reviews spread like wildfire all over the internet. Encourage your customers to talk about your company in their internet communities, online reviews, blog postings, comments, or forum threads. Many humans judge companies based on comments by other users or customers. This is because a comment via a past client has greater credibility in the eyes of a prospective customer than any marketing communications you may send out. All in all, whichever strategy you use, the secret lies in figuring out the strategies that paintings for you while keeping your options open to the different alternatives that are out there. Your success will depend on how much time you give to your campaign, in addition to your approach and commercial enterprise model.

7 Effective Tips That Help You With Your Lead Generation Strategy

Whether your marketing and income approach is evolved internally or externally, with these pointers you'll make certain that it's far both powerful and green:

1. Use the Correct Data For Best Targeting

If you have the right data, you can target the right audience. In reality, the more you already know approximately your target customers, the better you may goal them. Apart from this, communicating with your customers in the right tone is also very vital if you want them to pay interest to you.

2. Use Some Tools to Track Your Leads

Make sure you understand how to find out your ROI. Besides, you should set aside some money to measure and trace channels to attract your clients whether you are going to use your site, email, direct advertising or social media to attract them. With Google Analytics, for instance, you may identify the pages that are generating a good deal of traffic for you. You can also use other lead generation software as well.

three. Focus on Quality

This is obvious; however, most people just don't give any importance to this factor. Make certain you consciousness on quality alternatively of quantity. In other words, your income pressure shouldn't spend too much time on people who won't buy from you no matter what you do. You should only target capacity customers or clients.

4. Have a Solid Grading Structure

Your activity should have a strong structure, such as a short-term and a long-term campaign. This will help you think about one type of prospect at a time. Aside from this, you may want to have a criterion for finding out who may be your potential clients. It's also a great idea to nurture your leads. You should also teach your customers with useful information so they can understand your products higher.

5. Research Your Competition

You need to find out more about a product or provider that your competitors have launched lately. You should keep an eye on the activities of your competitors and use the information you collect to run circles around them.

6. Develop Relationships

You should aim high. You may want to create a list of customers that have gone through a change in occasions, like a merger or restructuring. Apart from this, you must make certain that you have a few massive organizations you may work with.

7. Use Your Website

You want traffic if you want to generate leads from your own business internet site. According to experts, you can use a number of techniques to make visitors click on your site. Below are primary strategies that can help a lot:

- Use paperwork: you can use forms to capture the data of your prospect customers. In precise, you may use smart forms to develop your database.

- Create an effective call-to-action (CTA): your CTAs should be effective enough to flip visitors into customers. This is the only way you could make more income.

Top Lead Sources to Grow Your Business

Studies show that the number one issue going through small and large enterprise owners these days isn't always having enough qualified potentialities. Every business proprietor would like to have more excellent prospects, but most either don't have the time or just do not have the expertise! In any given industry, there's a myriad of ability lead sources that can be used to supply your business with highly-qualified sales leads. Some are very simple and cheaper to set up, while others are more worried. Some will give you a trickle of leads; others will produce many leads.

In this chapter, we'll cover the best practices for lead generation that take the least amount of effort. You can pick out the ones you want to use for your own unique business needs.

What Would the "Ultimate" Lead Generation System Look Like?

A great lead technology system must have the following elements:

- Requires little manual effort to correctly run it, with the ability to be put almost entirely on "autopilot." This generates names, addresses, and even e-mail addresses of folks that respond and are interested by understanding more about your specific product or service.

- People who respond give you the permission to touch them and supply your fine sales presentation about your specific product or provider.

- Creates a positive relationship of agree with and generates a perception that you are "the" authority in your industry in regard in your product or service. (Tells your story.)

- Generates predictable results. The system works like a radio extent control that increases your business when grew to become up and continues your business when grew to become down.

The Top 6 Lead Generation Systems

1. Target Best Buyers

If you look at a financial statement that shows income generated from all your clients, you'll find that the "80/20 rule" works in your business. That is, just 20 percent of your customers are giving you 80 percent of the business and profitability. These are your "best buyers" or "dream clients".

What does this mean to you? It means that you should target and listen on these "best buyers" first due to the fact this can be the easiest way to grow your business and profitability. So take a few minutes now to create a profile of who your most "dream client" is.

2. Being Proactive With Your Leads is Your Key to Success

Most companies spend an enormous amount of time, attempt, and capital to get a few people from a massive target market a good way to "raise their hand" (respond) and become a new lead. Yet, most gained't invest time or attention to follow up in a diligent, well timed, and continuous manner. Every day that a lead goes unattended, you are eroding the viability of that opportunity by a huge amount. They would now not have responded and become a lead in the event that they were not interested in the advantage your product or service offers. The key to success with managing leads is to have an aggressive and proactive system in region, even if it's as simple as picking up the phone and calling your lead. Each new lead responded to you because they were involved, so pounce on each opportunity.

3. Direct Mail to Your Best Buyers

The fastest way to build your business is to target the best clients with a "laser-focused" approach that involves without delay mailing your "best buyers". This strategy alone has helped many businesses literally double their revenues in just 12 months (or less).

This disarmingly simple strategy is one of the maximum effective and least expensive ways to market and grow your business... Fast! Let me explain how:

Every market has what we call "best buyers." Those are the clients who will buy the maximum of what it is you offer. In essence, they are your "dream customers." Identify and select a goal group who will hear from you at least once in keeping with month. Most of the people on your list will throw the letter away the first four or five times they receive it, however remember that you are devoted to constructing a splendid reputation in the market, and gaining customers. It's a numbers game.

The first element you're going to do is to send them a letter introducing yourself and then deliver them an offer they cannot refuse. Then, send something out to these people every and each month, even if it's only a letter or a flyer offering a unfastened consultation or loose carrier of some kind. Over the next three hundred and sixty five days, those people are going to pay attention from you each and every month. And that's how they'll go from pronouncing "I've in no way heard of this organization before", to... "Who's this company I maintain hearing about", to... "Oh yeah, I've heard of (your company)", to... "Yes, we buy from them." Remember, this easy and inexpensive approach alone can growth your sales drastically. So, do it now, and do it consistently every single month!

4. Get Leads From Lead Brokers and Leads Companies

Another great manner to generate hot "geared up to buy" leads is to purchase them from lead brokers and lead companies. This employer's sole recognition is to generate leads and then sell them to businesses like you who want a great supply of consistent new business.

For example, consider there is a purchaser who is a very successful life insurance professional. His fundamental source of commercial enterprise and income comes from buying leads from the leads businesses. He continually buys leads from 3 different resources to keep his leads and sales numbers consistent. On common, each lead costs about $25 and he closes about 20% of the leads he buys. This method alone could make him a top producer that makes a totally nice dwelling for himself and his family. And those are surely practical effects to gain. So, if you don't presently purchase leads, including this strategy by myself can boom your business efficaciously.

5. Generate Leads From Internet Search Engines

One of the most powerful online strategies for generating leads is to draw targeted traffic to your website with the "pay-per-click" search engines (PPCSEs). PPCSEs can and need to turn out to be an vital part of your lead generating arsenal. PPCSEs allow you to faucet into the searches related to your industry and put your site at once in front of customers who are actively looking for what you're selling. You set your budget, set the price you're willing to pay for each sale lead and pay only when your clients click on via to your site. You are guaranteed to receive "hot possibilities" because you only pay for overall performance - pre-qualified clicks and visitors.

Here is an example of what can be finished with PPCSEs. The proprietor of a small, pretty-profitable software firm has built his commercial enterprise success almost entirely with only 2 advertising tools:

- Having a Website where he offers a free 30-day trial version of his software.

- Purchasing traffic from PPCSEs like Google AdWords.

He spends up to $three.50 per click for precisely-targeted keywords and makes a high go back on his investment. In fact, for every dollar he spends on keywords, he makes $5.00 to $7.00 back. This is approximately a 500-700% return on funding. Not horrific!

6. Advertise

Studies display that fifty% of all purchases is inspired via advertising. Advertising is also considered one of the best strategies a company can installation for producing leads. Plus, it's also a tremendous way to build name reputation in the market, which can get you publicity, "word-of-mouth" marketing, and different top notch benefits. Here are a few guidelines for running an marketing marketing campaign that has a high return on investment:

- Place ads in the most targeted publications your target marketplace reads.

- Consider less expensive ads in e-mail newsletters and websites that your target marketplace reads.

- Use direct response ads - constantly ask the reader of your ad to respond for more information by telephone, mail or via your website.

- Be proactive. Have a follow-up device in place to get most results from your advertising and marketing dollar.

- Use a compelling headline that introduces the biggest benefits your product or carrier offers in your client.

- Make them an offer that they'd be crazy to refuse so that they'll respond and become a brand new long-term purchaser.

Chapter 4: Do You Make These Lead Generation Mistakes?

There are some businesses out there that have been wondering all the while that because they have the high-quality lead generation campaign and they are utilizing it to the fullest, they will be earning more than what they are looking ahead to. However, this is not so, according to many commercial enterprise analysts and experts. Having one's own lead generation campaign to gather and generate marketing leads and sales leads is not the best way to financial success.

There are masses of mistakes that many companies can make when it comes to lead generation. For them, lead technology clearly approach opening up one's own business and watching for things to happen. Well, however definitely nothing will happen. If corporations really want to have some positive economic changes in their commercial enterprise(es), they should be very much aware of the following mistakes that many different companies have already committed and, quite frankly, maybe they have also made some or all of these mistakes when it comes to generating qualified leads.

Mistake #1: Not Having a Lead Generation System

One of the first mistakes they should be aware of in lead technology is not having a gadget in the first place. They may have one but it is not concrete and it doesn't virtually define the right way of remaining a sale. Some of these businesses that fall into this snare are the ones small businesses. They set up shop, open their doors and wait for things to happen. From what have been said, this kind of lead generation campaign will never make things happen. They may also have the best products and/or the pleasant services in the sector at a very affordable rate, however if the prospects or potential customers don't know they exist, these organizations won't still be in a position to sell whatever.

The only manner businesses can start promoting and incomes income is to make the public conscious of the existence of what they are offering. Why is it that some department shops and department stores, although they have been within the business for years, will still inform the public of new promotions? That's because the public is aware in their existence however they are not aware of what is being supplied on the present. For everyone to understand, they place their ads on TV, radio, and newspapers, and even engage in social media marketing. To have the right lead generation system is to promote product consciousness.

Mistake #2: Not Looking For the Right Sales Leads

Another mistake is that some agencies are not looking at the right sales leads. This one is without a doubt very simple to give an explanation for. Let's say a few companies have generated warm marketing and sales leads and they have deemed them as qualified leads. The things is, they are talking to the wrong people at the right time. The prospect they are talking to might not have the want for their products on the time and, therefore, they put that qualified lead aside wondering it's no longer a good lead.

Mistake #3: Only Using One Lead Generation Channel

Some corporations make the mistake of using only one single channel. One instance is telemarketing services. They make their human beings spend an excessive amount of time as professional appointment setters and they don't experiment on other channels which include social media marketing, email marketing or search engine marketing.

Mistake #4: Not Nurturing the Leads (or Not Knowing About the "How to")

Some businesses have gathered well-qualified leads but they don't know a way to nurture them. Maybe there are a few those who don't like to just accept unsolicited smartphone calls but they prefer and experience surfing social media sites like Twitter, LinkedIn, and Facebook, while others enjoy checking their emails from time to time. These are some of the mistakes most companies make. They can accumulate warm qualified leads but they don't know what to do with it. Others simply just don't have the manpower and facilities to carry out lead generation campaigns. Fortunately, there are many one-of-a-kind B2B lead generation companies to outsource lead generation marketing services.

Chapter 5: Generating Leads With Blogging

If you wish to offer your website online's search engine rating an increase and enhance the quantity of natural leads that you get, then you need to establish an SEO method.

A overall search engine marketing method includes numerous elements, together with improving your websites, keyword studies, backlinking, and most drastically, producing top excellent material which each search engines like google and yahoo and your audience are going to like. Among the appropriate strategies to set up shareable and linkable content is via running a blog.

Blog web sites are content material management structures that are both on your primary website, or in a subdomain or subdirectory, and they consist of numerous capabilities inclusive of RSS feeds, remarks and trackbacks. What extremely few individuals recognize are the blessings they could get with the aid of having an optimized weblog, consisting of suitable material. When it concerns producing more leads, there are masses of advantages which you may acquire from optimizing your weblog web page.

Have Fresh Content for a Better Ranking

When you constantly enhance the cloth to your site, you increase your odds of ranking higher on Google and other search engines. Your business weblog site gives a notable method to be able to renew and enhance your internet site continuously. Not just is this going to help to bring in and keep customers on your website evidently, but, the hunt engine bots likewise like web sites with new fabric.

By now, it ought to be rather apparent that content is king, when it concerns search engine optimization. All of the correct SEO techniques are based upon producing first-rate material. Appropriate and sparkling cloth is useful to customers and is going to help in cultivating hobby in your product or service amongst prospective clients.

How to Have More Control Over the Content

When you have got the capability to create extra helpful, unique fabric in your weblog website online, you've got overall manipulate over the message that you are attempting to provide to your target market about your services or products. With search engine marketing optimization, you continue to be in whole manipulate of your key phrases, further to the links that you installed your posts. Continuously offering sparkling material for your weblog web page offers you considerable electricity over your net visibility.

Have Better Internal Linking

This benefit of a very optimized weblog website is linked to having higher manipulate of your on line visibility. With the capability to manage the content that you placed on your weblog site, you can select to link to various portions of your weblog posts to the numerous pages to your site making use of the anchor text that you select. Not simply does this form of linking inform the numerous search engines like google and yahoo what to search for on your website, but, it likewise directs feasible customers in your sales or landing pages.

How to Draw In Inbound Hyperlinks More Easily

Among the maximum essential factors that you need to reflect onconsideration on whilst it pertains to search engine rating is backlinking. When Google's bots find out a domain with out back-links, it instantly presumes that the website has little to provide. Nevertheless, a site which has loads of one way links is most probably to be ranked a lot higher within the engines like google because of the fact that it possibly consists of useful cloth.

It is essential to don't forget, despite the fact that, is that the one-way links need to simply be from associated or extraordinarily favored web sites. If your website includes quite a few backlinks which aren't suitable, it'd land up being punished.

This is wherein you may drastically take gain of hosting a blog website. Not simply does every submit that you produce offer involved visitors with a hyperlink which they are able to share, however, you may likewise produce one way links your self by sharing some of your posts with your social networks.

Your traffic are going to constantly percentage numerous posts more than others, so very well monitoring the posts is going to, over time, provide you a far higher idea of the form of material that you should be generating to your target market.

Have More Variety

Because on-line search engines are looking for fabric which goes to be useful for users, you're alternatively restricted regarding simply how plenty content material you may have on your primary commercial enterprise web site. Nevertheless, in case you host a blog site, it's far going to can help you write about whatever which you feel your audience goes to advantage from, which is going to assist them to determine on whether to buy your products or services, in spite of whether or not the fabric fits inside your sitemap.

It is extraordinarily incredible that you could put 'how-to' or list posts to your primary internet site, yet these have definitely proven to be among the maximum prominent topics searched for on-line. Blogging assists to healthy the content that's often looked for on-line whilst supporting to enhance the possible quantity of click-throughs which you get from your content.

Release Content Which Would Damage Your Ranking Otherwise

Along with developing ordinary posts, blogging software program is ideal whilst you want to rank higher on the web seek engine and acquire links to particular kinds of fabric which may in the end harm your number one internet site's search engine marketing. These encompass frequently asked questions, newsletter records, item updates, and online media rooms. Hosting a blog website online isn't always simply going to shape a vital a part of your total search engine marketing and lead era method, however, it's far likewise an fantastic approach to beautify your trustworthiness and offer your enterprise a tailor-made voice.

search engine marketing is the Key

According to a present day studies observe accomplished via HubSpot, 3-quarters of people never ever scroll beyond the initial web page of the search consequences. Investing numerous hours composing, rewording, and enhancing your content, for it to collect dust on the second web page of Google might be a harsh truth to swallow.

If you desire to enhance your seek ranking, then you definately want to pay attention on developing an exceedingly optimized blog website online with search engine optimization in mind. It starts offevolved with coming across your greatest opportunities which exist for doing so, with the potential to yield great outcomes in your search rating, which consequently goes to help in generating greater ready leads.

Recognize Authoritative Hyperlinks

Page authority is a metric that is determined by using nearly every search engine optimization device, and it determines how properly a selected page to your website would possibly rank in a search. There are masses of numerous components which can effect this, inclusive of distinct IPs linking to a particulatwebsite, the amount of incoming links, and precise domains. The more the web page authority, the greater possibly that page goes to rank higher inside the online search engine.

The excessive authority pages can likewise help in enhancing the rating of other pages to your website, involving the ones which are currently ranking on the second web page of Google, with the aid of just linking to them. Initially, you have to recognize your most dependable pages. This can be accomplished by using utilising tools which includes Moz's Open Site Explorer.

Recognize Valuable Keywords

Now that you apprehend where your pages rank, you are going to have to expose high-placed key phrases which line up with your excessive authority pages. You can utilize Google Analytics and filter out all of the key phrases you currently rank for in descending order. Filter your seek by way of everything which suggests up in a position above 10, that's the preliminary web page of search effects, to determine your best possibilities for reinforcing your rank.

Take Action

When you have truly found your high authority websites and the valuable key phrases, you could utilize this information to enhance the hunt ranking of the remainder of your web sites, by means of making use of long-tail keywords to link to appropriate pages in your website. Include a appropriate hyperlink out of your high authority pages to other pages for your web page to beautify your search ranking, however, it's far going to likewise boost your reader's enjoy without interrupting the reader's revel in by packing quite a few unimportant key phrases for your maximum critical pages.

A commercial enterprise blog site goes to supply you with plenty of precise blessings, but, you need to be certain to hold it out in a smart way, and you need to be prepared to vicinity inside the work of optimizing your blog website and rejuvenating your blog web page's cloth often. Nevertheless, putting in the time to guarantee you devote to the process of running a blog goes to deliver you with a vast advantage.

A community of bloggers is going to provide you the contextual back-links which might be normally presented with the aid of engines like google by using ranking your internet site higher. Routine readers of your weblog site are going to generally supply a lift on your web page's publicity by sharing gadgets of hobby, particularly on social networks.

Building Relationships with Social Networks

In case your organization is working on a price range plan, it could normally be a hurdle to relate the attempt which you are making an investment in constructing relationships on social networks with the real ROI. If you've got clearly been devoting a incredible deal of time on social networks, however, do now not believe that you are obtaining the effects that you expect, you may begin to question whether the efforts which you are placing in are genuinely the best method to make investments your finite assets and time.

Regrettably, absolutely few individuals have the capability to discover the definitive response to the questions they have in their minds, and that makes them extra unwilling to jump onto what they view because the "Social Media Bandwagon." While several businesses see the severa social network platforms as a viable and essential marketing channel for his or her business, others see it as a yet unforeseeable and unverified diversion that doesn't sincerely lend itself to traditional metrics. Nevertheless, that is sincerely now not correct.

Make Friends on Social Media

For severa agencies who are seeking to create more leads at the internet, social networks supply many sturdy and special benefits, consisting of the increased exposure in their brand names, providing more big insights into client behavior, and supporting in growing greater powerful relationships with their clients. By doing this, attractive with consumers and the target market through social networks has without a doubt turned into one of the maximum critical pillars of any powerful net advertising technique. While preserving this in mind, right here are the various maximum a success social network practices that can assist your business to increase search engine marketing efforts, broaden engagement, and effect the bottom line of your enterprise by means of helping you to provide a extensive amount of leads.

Organically Boost Your Following

The followers and enthusiasts which you get via social networks and the connections which you make thru these systems can also have a great effect for your fashionable rating on Google and other search engines.

While growing a sturdy social network following in an organic way is a technique that may require a while, it may deliver you with an exceedingly useful increase to your lead technology and enterprise if you may hold being regular. This shows having the capability to hold a voice that is awesome to your business whilst you are offering your lovers the normal product and standing updates.

To take benefit of your social media networks, you need to set up your self and your business as extremely responsive, by means of constantly making positive you post beneficial suggestions, nonetheless being open to questions, sharing beneficial blog web page posts, and normally publishing popular gadgets of hobby in your goal marketplace. Ensure which you have the ability to observe this up via enticing together with your target marketplace in direct discussions.

Open and direct discussions and engagements with clients are going to make certain which you have the capability to hold an interactive and big following considering that your present lovers and followers are going to be inspired to go back. Social network likewise allows you to expand subject matter authority that is going to in the end reason you to usher in more fans and fans, and that is going to reinforce your prospective leads.

Motivate External Sites to Link to Your Content

Among the most sizeable blessings which you can collect from related to social community engagement inside your net advertising method is that it makes it loads easier to get external links to your sites from various various sources. When you may involve range with your inbound hyperlinks, it is able to increase your search ranking on Google and drastically broaden your authority at the net.

Nevertheless, in order so as to accumulate various incoming hyperlinks on your internet site from extremely dependable sources, you need to initially have pinnacle great, useful, fresh, and reliable fabric in your internet site.

Presuming that the content material on your weblog and site is particular and beneficial, you need to have the ability to make use of this as bait, whilst your social networks are the fishing rod that ensures your bait gets put ahead of your target marketplace, which can also then be utilized to draw enthusiasts and fans.

Post Optimization

While the optimization of your posts on social networks is substantially dependent on the pre-existing cloth which you are sharing, it can likewise supply you with the danger of producing a second seek channel. Along with list information articles and know-how chart entries, Google generally capabilities social community updates and posts on pinnacle of its on-line search engine seek pages.

While this is absolutely a short-term inspiration, making sure that every one your posts on social networks are absolutely greater is going to guarantee that you have the capability to capitalize in this.

To do this, you are going to first of all require something that you may utilize to anchor your post. This might be whatever of interest on your audiences, consisting of an infographic, a link to a publish, or an embedded video. Whatever you choose to make use of, this is going to be the shape which you require to identify descriptively and properly, using key phrases to make certain that it is going to have a much better possibility of rating in searches.

Motivate More Individuals to Share Your Posts

Just as getting outside links in your internet site provides in your emblem name's internet authority, so does social sharing. When Google and the other search engines discover symptoms that there are legitimate outside hints of the cloth you publish on social networks, your odds are more to get a skyward bump on your domain authority.

If 10 people share one in every of your posts with their social community, it is brilliant, but, you wish to be going for masses of shares. Although charming or useful posts are going to continuously have a handful of individuals sharing them with their social community, the best method in an effort to get the numbers you require to make a distinction is to enchantment straight for your lovers.

This will be within the shape of a praise, like a loose object, an entry right into a drawing for a reward, or anything else that you accept as true with may also encourage your lovers and fans to percentage your posts with their social media.

Having a properly-planned-out method for your interactions on the severa social network structures is going to enable you to hastily share your fabric at the same time as you likewise construct one-way links on your website online. Social networks can likewise be applied to reinforce your material by means of making it a point of verbal exchange amongst your followers and enthusiasts, that's ultimately going to help you in developing a greater effective dating in among your logo call and your goal market.

Link to Prospective Clients By Having Good search engine marketing

Many people have clearly devoted years of their lives on the computer systems and feature genuinely lived for quite a chunk inside the records technology, consequently, extremely few people ever prevent to admire how quick the net is and the way crucial it's miles for enterprise. With trillions of pages of their indexes, it's far actually terrific that engines like google are able to locating pages with responses to a specific search inquiry in a matter of nanoseconds.

As a be counted of truth, absolutely 25 years earlier, you would have needed to visit a library and commit hours to pouring via the cardboard catalog and the dewy decimal machine to discover a response on your questions that Google is able to now provide you in a heartbeat. This fast get entry to to records has really converted how we get entry to the facts we require each day.

search engine marketing is absolutely nothing more than 'opposite-engineering' the method of exploring those trillions of websites to find out the information that we require. By ensuring that your website may be quick browsed and accessed by means of search bots, that it fulfills the necessities which can be set out by using the online search engine for reliable and beneficial data, and that it consists of useful fabric on your site visitors, you are going to be positive that any seek of your goal phrases and keywords is going to have you ranking well on Google and other search engines like google.

search engine optimization is Even Better for Businesses That Don't Have Websites

In the thoughts of the bulk of humans, SEO is taken into consideration as an online tool which completely handles web sites, but, its importance is going some distance beyond that. Considering that on-line search engines get their information from different sources apart from web sites, your enterprise can substantially take benefit of exposure if it takes place to seem among the preliminary outcomes confirmed on the search page.

For instance, masses of folks who search for organizations, products or services on Google from their mobile phones are searching for instructions or touch numbers. If your enterprise is cited in a directory site along with Google My Business, the Yellow Pages, LinkedIn, or similar databases, you can be discovered on Google in spite of having or now not having a commercial enterprise internet site.

In fact, having a Google My Business listing, similarly to Google Maps, can make it relatively easy for companies with out a website to be located unexpectedly on the web search engine. Having a list on Google My Business enables you to include electronic mail address, a contact variety, an outline of your business, alongside the descriptions of the products and services which you offer. Google makes use of this statistics that it acquires from its network to consist of purchaser critiques, guidelines, and maps.

As along with your web site, you could optimize those listings by way of such as pertinent key phrases to the description of your business, which is going to permit your enterprise to be cited better within the seek engine end result when a probable client is attempting to find a specific provider.

The Worth of SEO

If you had to determine, might you instead purchase a $one hundred seventy,000 Honda, or a $2 hundred,000 Ferrari? The reason why you are greater likely to pick out the Ferrari, even though it fees greater, is that it gives you a more experience of really worth. In numerous methods, optimizing your website online is a tad like that.

Sure, it's miles going to fee you much less money and time to purchase ads and achieve more effects in the shape of leads, visits, pins, likes, and retweets, but, few of these are going to land up converting into actual paying clients. Search engine optimization goals folks who are currently considering obtaining something product or service you are presenting and all they need to do is find out you, and for you to persuade them that you are their greatest alternative.

Achieve a Greater Return on Investment

search engine optimization and normally all styles of online marketing are going to produce a more ROI for your business than their offline equivalents. This is especially due to the truth which you do now not should head out and try to seize the attention of a capability customer.

Rather, with SEO, purchasers themselves are routing incoming visitors in your internet site. This assists you in acquiring a far higher economic investment to go back margin to your item placements and advertisements. With SEO, you could effects maintain a watch on the charge of your conversions and simply just how a whole lot site visitors organic keywords and searches are helping you in pushing in your pages. You actually have the opportunity of defining or specifying your conversions. Search engine optimization offers you the capability to reveal your conversions in regards to leads or visits.

More Exposure

With search engine marketing, you may decorate your on line exposure, which is going to equate to more leads and plenty higher sales margins. Every wonderful online marketer is familiar with that content is king as it is what pushes consumers on your enterprise. If you have pinnacle-satisfactory fabric, it's far going to maintain your clients and readers hooked, but, it can not continually equate to a greater ranking on Google. Nevertheless, with on line search engine enhanced content material, your cloth may end up being greater sizeable to your readers and goal market.

Research study has truely verified that lots of human beings do now not make it past the preliminary pages of the search engine end result, which indicates if you want to rank higher so your goal market can also find out you, then you definately want to enhance your fabric. A clever search engine marketing approach is going to assist you to rank higher on Google when your keywords are browsed. SEO assists in keeping your business famous inside the mind of viable customers.

Get Better Coverage

Life is swiftly heading digital, and while TV, radio, and print are going to keep on being supplied, more organizations are going to depend upon the Web to marketplace their company. Search engine optimization can also help in presenting you lots better coverage which goes to let you attain your goal market, anywhere they're inside the world.

With billions of searches accomplished every day on Google and different on-line search engine, improving your fabric for SEO is going to imply that you can attain more people. If your gadgets and articles are well optimized, extra people are going to peer it, which is going to equate to extra leads.

Establish Credibility

Users, specifically folks that are trying to find a selected kind of services or products are maximum possibly to carry out more than one search, the use of severa keywords. If you've got genuinely efficaciously optimized your website online's fabric, it's miles extra possibly to seem higher within the results.

When your website seems excessive up on the SERP for numerous searches within the same niche, possible readers and customers are sure to take your website more severely and view you as an expert on the difficulty that you're going over. Appear excessive up on the online seek engine for numerous search terms, brings extra self-self assurance and faith to your target market and readers. With trustworthiness comes greater visibility, publicity, or even a viable bargaining chip in case you are performing any offline negotiations with a likely purchaser.

A Cost-Effective Marketing Approach

If you are making unique errors for your SEO technique, it is able to wind up costing you with the aid of keeping your website online concealed in obscurity. Nevertheless, whilst performed nicely, search engine marketing is most of the maximum low priced kinds of internet advertising and marketing which your enterprise may additionally use. When your search engine marketing is particularly targeted at boosting your natural seek end result ratings, it wishes actually few economic charges.

Actually, if you have a sturdy draw close of search engine optimization, you might wind up no longer having to invest any coins whatsoever. Paired with its broad reach, SEO advertising might be most of the most low-cost forms of advertising and marketing presented to push greater visitors and create extra leads.

It is as a substitute tremendous that irrespective of all of its benefits, SEO nonetheless isn't always completely utilized by numerous on-line marketers and corporations. Nevertheless, in case you aren't improving your site and material, you'll be losing on a lots of business and falling in the back of the competition.

SEO is such an crucial approach for developing more leads and enhancing your presence on the net; it's far crucial that, in case you are not presently using this useful and low-price device, that you begin executing an search engine optimization advertising technique these days.

Utilize Webinars to Establish The Position of an Expert

Among the most remarkable traits amongst effective internet online entrepreneurs that has clearly sincerely began to emerge during the last severa years is the addition of webinars in their advertising and sales campaigns. A webinar is a type of stay workshop or presentation that is held online. Presently, those styles of workshops are finishing up being a very popular channel for the advertising and flow of different services and products.

If you have got virtually ever long gone to a workshop, then you have to be pretty acquainted with the primary layout of the occasion that normally consists of a mediator, guests, several people who are at the back of the presentations, and a q&a consultation in which individuals have the opportunity to study extra.

The purpose for the currently determined webinar achievement is due to the raise in customer options for actual-time video. If you are not the use of webinars in your present internet advertising and marketing initiatives, right here are the various benefits that have really made website hosting webinars so outstanding over the last severa years with net entrepreneurs.

Present Yourself and Your Business Personally

There are countless potential purchasers, companions and companies situated around the world who recognise not anything about you, however, who most probable need to. Anybody who might benefit from the products and services which you provide ought to have a easy technique to learn extra approximately you.

Even though social community systems which includes Facebook and professional networking web sites consisting of LinkedIn supply super contact factors, they are restrained. A webinar goes to permit you to have a greater individualized path closer to your target market and allow you to speak about your object and yourself.

Show Your Authority and Trustworthiness

Hosting a live webinar, while contrasted to a pre-recorded video, assists in seeing who's a expert and who's a phony. A live webinar substances you with a platform in which you can individually display that you have competence and revel in in your subject and which you should be checked out as an authority to your market.

Nevertheless, you want to make sure about what you are discussing, or people who attend your webinar are going to hastily see via you.

Offer Your Services And Products in a Less Salesy Manner

The important recognition of a stay webinar isn't always the apparent using of sales, but instead, to inform your target market about your products or services.

Nevertheless, income can arise from evidently displaying your reliability, supplying your target market vital info, and speaking about your products or services as a part of the discussion. You may also even have publish-event interactions with your participants in that can pass an extended manner in sustaining your income cycle with out being extraordinarily competitive.

Generate Leads and Broaden the Sales Funnel

Webinars are classified as event advertising and marketing; nonetheless, it is a important advertising region wherein lots of people inside the market will be predisposed to exclude out in their tactical advertising and marketing strategies. Nevertheless, that is a large error because of the fee and effect which online event advertising has on different factors of net marketing.

Broaden Your Mailing Lists and Your Network

Almost all of the webinar systems which you could make use of use email to sign on the contributors, which suggests that you can swiftly assemble your e-mail lists with the aid of without delay acquiring visitor's e-mails after they sign on. While the people may not be truly registering for your agencies' subscriber list, you can encompass them and offer a possibility to unsubscribe every time they choice.

The technique to do this is to have an choose-in checkbox with a blub specifying that they're going to be protected to your publication if they do now not uncheck the box. This is a quick method to collect more clients and produce in extra leads.

Lower Your Expenditures As You Are Offering a Practical Method to Meet

It is a truth that hosting an offline occasion may cost a little you substantially greater coins. To begin, while you host an offline occasion, you want to cope with the expense of the region, leaflet printing, and different stationery, and convey beverages. With on-line activities, along with a webinars, the fees are little or no, because of the fact which you do no longer want to spend for the overhead of website hosting the occasion.

Webinars are likewise clearly sensible for the guests due to the fact they do no longer want to take time out in their day to trip there. Additionally, on line events may additionally convey in contributors from all around the planet, instead of in reality to your area, due to the fact that they just require a proper internet connection to head there.

Boost Your Bottom Line

All of the above factors of webinars have clear sales advantages for your business. This is on the grounds that individuals are going to gladly invest their coins in products or services which might be offered by way of folks that they accept as true with and recognize. For this clean cause, delivering your informative material and income via webinars is a outstanding approach to create leads and assemble your commercial enterprise based totally upon these advantages on my own. The bright aspect, nonetheless, is the truth that webinars may additionally do a lot more.

When you study, talk approximately, and sell your service or product via a webinar, you are ensured to see a boost in leads and eventually income. By appearing demonstrations for the guests and permitting them to invite questions on your shows, they may collect a better comprehension of the products or services you are imparting and are going to be happier to purchase from you.

The questions requested and the responses of folks that are attending your webinar can likewise offer you the useful information which you can utilize in destiny advertising tasks. Plus, income pitches which might be provided at webinars commonly have greater conversion costs contrasted to item launches or income letters by myself.

Because of the Web, it's far now completely viable to have actual-time video connections with your goal marketplace irrespective of wherein in the world they live. For online marketers who host professional occasions in which a easy video chat certainly will not suffice, a live webinar is what you need to be the use of.

Use Email Marketing to Get More Leads

Email advertising has honestly swiftly changed into one of the vital guns for corporations and online entrepreneurs alike. You might be questioning what it is why e-mail marketing affords this type of massive advantage over more general advertising strategies and why it can provide you a much better return for your monetary investments and supply you with greater effective metrics to evaluate purchaser engagement.

When it worries e-mail advertising projects, they have actually specific blessings wherein may additionally assist in bringing in greater leads and growing your brand name.

Less Time And Effort Are Needed

To get a proper concept of really just how lots time you may conserve with an electronic mail advertising and marketing marketing campaign, you simply need to evaluate this approach to 2 other common marketing techniques which might be often used by direct-to-consumer interactions and direct-to-commercial enterprise.

- Printed mailers: no longer simply do you need to devote the time waiting on a image clothier to produce your mailer, frequently needing a number of changes, however, you likewise want to allow time for transport.

- Telesales campaigns: this marketing approach needs that you reserve a while to supply a script and watch for your sales department to undergo the prolonged call list.

Email advertising, but, allows you to generate marketing content fairly rapidly and offer it to your consumers, feasible clients, and target marketplace, in less than a couple of hours.

Real-Time Interaction

Printed mailers and telesales have a prolonged period in between the preliminary improvement of the marketing campaign and its execution. This means that these strategies are going to just work for lengthy-tail campaigns which might be going to allow the sluggish transport of these unique marketing strategies.

Because you can finish and ship out a advertising email in more than one hours, it's far definitely feasible to ship out mailers for your target market which marketplace products or services that you want to launch the identical day. An electronic mail goes to even allow you to send out tailor-made actual-time messages which show up in purchaser's inboxes on their birthdays or anniversaries.

Customize Your Message

Print, TV, radio, and telesales campaigns are specially carried out with a one-size-suits-all technique. This makes it difficult to goal precise clients with a tailor-made message. This differs from electronic mail advertising, which components you with a dynamic approach to marketplace offers in your goal marketplace.

Not simply does this technique allow you to ship out a message which includes the prospect's name, however, you may likewise supply more details consisting of their buy records. The customization of e mail advertising messages is likewise some distance more easy than sending out a personalized postal or print mailer. Consequently, it's far viable to additionally split your mailing listing into tinier customer lists for extra customization.

Categorize Your User Data

Email advertising and marketing likewise permits you to categorize your number one mailing list into even tinier lists that are going to let you send out extremely targeted messages on your goal marketplace. With extraordinarily customized and focused messages, you will drastically raise your price of conversions of your leads because of the fact that the message they get is extraordinarily particular to them.

For instance, in case you are a florist, you can positioned within the time to browse your database to discover all of your purchasers who've definitely formerly bought daffodils from your enterprise. You may additionally then utilize this targeted information to send out these customers an e-mail in April when the deliveries of daffodils are at their greatest. In this example, you're going to send your electronic mail messages to those consumers who are greater than in all likelihood to do so by means of buying.

Send Out More Regular Communications

Because an e mail does no longer take as long to expand and ship out as different advertising and marketing channels, you have got the capability to have interaction together with your customers and goal market more often. Instead of being confined to 1 leaflet monthly or quarterly, you can quickly produce and ship a advertising and marketing e-mail each week.

Naturally, you could even send out e mail messages extra often when you have the authorization of your clients. Nevertheless, you need to take into account that it's also recommended that you stay clean of sending out an e mail to consumers multiple time every week until it's far simply needed.

Lower Overhead

A legitimate e mail advertising marketing campaign might be accomplished at a portion of the cost of other strategies. It isn't always important to have a crowd of market professionals, designers, and other employees when you are handling email marketing campaigns.

Additionally, you do now not want to worry approximately advertising quotes, mailing costs, smartphone strains or printing. Actually, you could now fast discover email advertising services that are going to offer you professional e mail design templates which you may swiftly customize to suit your requirements.

Streamlined Tracking

If you need to get functional and specific monitoring records out of your advertising campaign, there are multiple options which might be more effective than electronic mail advertising. Having this information handy is going to allow you swiftly examine what works to decide and produce in capacity customers and what does now not work. Expert e-mail platforms may also deliver you with actual-time details concerning who opened your e mail message, if they click the hyperlink in the message, similarly to permitting you recognize how many people claimed that your message was junk mail.

Superior Brand Name Acknowledgment

A few of the most identifiable brand names international are so famous that they are associated with the marketplace in which they run. Take Spotify, as an example, all of the emails which they ship to their subscribers and customers are remarkably curated and applicable.

Email advertising campaigns are a exquisite technique to establish your logo call identification considering the fact that they offer you a straight line to the inboxes of your potential consumers. When you begin to produce essential cloth in your client, you will acquire a small edge over your competitors and produce more leads of individuals who may be considering shopping for your services or products.

The best part of email marketing is that you can likewise utilize your emails to acquire beneficial feedback from your customers. You may find out if your client is satisfied with the cloth that you are providing, or in the event that they wish to find out some thing one-of-a-kind.

Learning this data can allow you to extra successfully tailor your advertising task to fulfill the necessities of your target marketplace, which may cause your business creating additional leads.

Develop More Powerful Consumer Relationships

Customers cost an superb e mail, and the time and effort that you spend money on getting ready the appropriate e-mail will not move undetected. Much of your potential customers and gift clients wish to recognize what's taking vicinity for your business and what they'll do to get blanketed. While it's miles nearly unbelievable to hook up with all your customers by using cellphone or head to head, you could reach all of them unexpectedly with a very good marketing marketing campaign. You may also even establish a drip marketing campaign to assist you in improving the method.

Drip e-mail marketing initiatives are continuous and are going to power the consumer down the client's adventure to the final sale. They are normally applied to provide goal market with continuous really worth whilst helping in keeping your emblem name on pinnacle of your customers' minds. Many times, you could set up those campaigns as much as steadily "drip" handy info, tips or gadgets, over a number of days, weeks, or months.

Boost Your Site Traffic

Emails are a splendid method to obtain more traffic in your internet site. You can comprise pertinent hyperlinks in your website inside the frame of the email. You can also likewise make use of your e-mail advertising and marketing initiatives to get your purchasers to engage with different incredible pieces of cloth which you have to your site or your blog web page. Ensure that you function social sharing buttons to your emails to inspire your customers to promote your fabric throughout their very own social channels.

It can be clean to get wrapped up in the complexities of growing an email marketing marketing campaign this is going to paintings on your enterprise and your customers. There is a remarkable deal of learning included, but, there's likewise a exquisite deal of probabilities to engage and interact with your purchasers, in place of sincerely sending them emails constantly.

With e mail advertising and marketing, you could establish your logo name, establish yourself as a seasoned, and convey more leads, with out breaking your spending plan.

By now, it must be apparent how electronic mail advertising may also extensively advantage your commercial enterprise in preference to other traditional advertising channels. Integrating e mail advertising into your total advertising technique goes to offer you a completely unique benefit over your competition, enable you to set up relationships together with your goal market, and deliver you with the metrics and information which you require to beautify your advertising tasks and convey in extra leads.

Chapter 6: What Is Linkedin?

LinkedIn is an interpersonal organization for professionals to accomplice, percentage, and examine. It's like Facebook on your vocation. In spite of being quite probably the maximum well-known social ranges today, severa man or woman sincerely haven't any clue approximately what LinkedIn have to be applied for or how they may benefit from being on it. You can develop your corporation more by way of buying an ever increasing range of advantages.

Whether you're a showcasing leader at a widespread enterprise, an entrepreneur who runs a touch community keep or maybe a first-12 months undergrad looking for their first career next to graduating, LinkedIn is for everybody and each and each character who's eager on drawing close their expert lifestyles extra in a serious manner by trying to find new possibilities to increase their vocations and to accomplice with distinctive professionals.

You can recall LinkedIn the reducing aspect likeness going to a customary structures administration occasion in which you continue to satisfy specific professionals face to face, speak a tad approximately what you do, and alternate commercial enterprise cards. It's like one primary virtual systems administration event.

On LinkedIn, you community with individuals by means of including them as 'institutions,' like how you'd make a associate call for on Facebook. You talk through personal message (or on hand contact records), and you've the whole lot of your professional enjoy and accomplishments unfold out in a superbly coordinated profile to flaunt to unique customers.

LinkedIn is like Facebook as far as its format and expansive component offering. These factors are greater unique given that they deal with specialists, yet by means of and big, within the event which you recognize how to make use of Facebook or some other similar casual community, LinkedIn is to some degree tantamount. Prior to shifting onto the method that how you can carry in cash, let take a look at the primary factors of linkedIn. It is fundamental in mild of the fact that your way towards blessings relies upon on the way you utilize the application and also you cannot utilize the software until you understand about its highlights.

LinkedIn's Main Features

Here are a portion of the essential factors that this business network offers and the way they've been intended to be used by professionals. Amateurs can likewise get profited from it.

Home: Once you've signed in to LinkedIn, the house channel is your information source, displaying ongoing posts from your institutions with one-of-a-kind experts and buddies pages you are following.

Profile: Your profile shows your call, your photo, your place, your profession and all the extra right at the top. Beneath that, you can modify distinctive diverse segments like a short outline, work insight, training and specific segments in basically the same manner to how you could make a traditional resume or CV.

My Network: Here you may take a look at a rundown of the relative multitude of specialists you're at present related to on LinkedIn. Assuming you go with the flow your mouse over this preference within the top menu, you may likewise have the choice to see diverse specific alternatives a good way to permit you to upload contacts, have a look at people you is probably conscious and song down graduated class.

Occupations: such positions postings are posted on LinkedIn regularly through agencies, and LinkedIn will prescribe explicit positions to you in view of your present records, including your vicinity and discretionary work inclinations that you may finish up to land better-custom-made position postings.

Interests: notwithstanding your associations with professionals, you can comply with precise interests on LinkedIn also. These contain corporation pages, bunches as indicated by using location or hobby, LinkedIn's Slide Share degree for slideshow dispensing and LinkedIn's Lynda level for instructive functions.

Search bar: LinkedIn has a robust inquiry include that allows you to channel your effects down as indicated by using some different adaptable fields. Click "Progressed" alongside the pursuit bar to song down unambiguous experts, companies, occupations after which a few.

Messages: When you want to begin a dialogue with every other professional, you can do as such by way of sending them a personal message thru LinkedIn.

You can likewise upload connections, comprise snap shots after which some.

Warnings: Like different casual corporations, LinkedIn has a note include that tells you when you've been supported through someone, welcome to sign up for something or invited to observe a submit you'll be eager on.

Forthcoming Invitations: When special experts welcome you to interface with them on LinkedIn, you'll get a greeting that you will need to recommend.

How to Kick Off on LinkedIn?

Prior to persevering with on the ways that how you could deliver in coins for your self or to your association, it's miles vital to see that how you may start your presence on LinkedIn. Following are the courses via which you could reason a solid presence and could to have high-quality possibilities purchasing more blessings.

Monetization

1. Develop your LinkedIn profile: You cannot move without delay from "important LinkedIn profile" to "profitable device." Baby steps. To start with, you really need to make your LinkedIn profile as entire as might be anticipated, along with adding a brand new, appealing image and carrying out the immeasurably good sized professional portfolio phase. A resume lets people recognise what you've performed; a portfolio demonstrates it. When you've got this finished, do not forget to:

Post each day in any occasion. Assuming you really need to, use HootSuite to plan a whole week of posts ahead of time.

2. Recount a Brand Story: Your LinkedIn profile can not appear as though you'll acknowledge any vintage work or possibility. You need to it appears that evidently make a brand tale - a task for your self or your commercial enterprise. You're now not trusting that your career will occur; you're as of now making

extraordinary development to date, most of the manner to conducting a particular objective.

Add your LinkedIn identification on your organisation website online, any vicinity you painting your center assignment. Additionally, make sure to encompass any LI patron surveys you get.

three. Structure connections: I realize you've got in all likelihood not noted a ton of those "Challenge to interface on LinkedIn" messages. You've probably likewise not noted the "So and new function" messages. Time to dive into your e mail files and begin answering. The extra associations you've got, and the extra you collaborate with those associations, the extra grounded your LinkedIn network becomes. It's likewise crucial to compose and request pointers - in addition to the "embraced talents" kind, however the real composed proposals that show up on your profile. These help with demonstrating which you are dependable and that you have strong associations with preceding and cutting-edge partners.

Make LinkedIn bunches wherein your goal market connects with, have a look at and partake in their associations to see what styles of topics are drawing commitment. Address those topics to your company circulation.

Transfer severa full-size files always (not in reality pictures on occasion pdfs, recordings, and infographics continuously) and hold it coordinated. Get clarification on some matters and preserve challenges utilising Targeted posts for pick crowds.

four. Influence your appealing object or management: There are numerous methods of bringing in cash on LinkedIn, but the first and handiest way is often to make a marketable item. Many people decide to conform facts items, as an instance, persuasive advisers for final results in their picked fields or how-to specialized manuals for his or her situation topics. Data gadgets are notable coins generators considering they're nearly usually automatic (virtual books, PDFs, and so on), implying that they don't fee loads of coins to produce or shipping. Other attractive items include published replica books in addition to items related straightforwardly on your business. Assuming you sell customized shoes, as an example, ensure individuals can purchase your object by means of clicking to your save from your LinkedIn profile.

5. Offer counseling administrations: If you have mastery in a selected location, make certain your LinkedIn associations realise which you offer counseling administrations. Many people make a variety of additional cash always by way of conversing with special agencies or business human beings approximately what they've realized. Assuming you go the advisor course, make certain it's miles completely integrated into your photograph - you do not agree with every body have to consider you're hustling for expert positions essentially in mild of the reality that you really need some additional money.

How to Make Money the usage of LinkedIn?

LinkedIn is the principle informal community for professionals, so generally, it tends to be an extraordinary interpersonal enterprise to use to produce pay in diverse methods. We understand you've got perused a variety of stuff that the way to begin bringing in cash at the linkedln with the aid of fostering a decent profile, so we can keep away from all of that and make a plunge directly into approaches you can utilize LinkedIn to herald coins on line via developing your mailing list, selling gadgets, presenting administrations, tracking down publicists, increasing book deals, advancing offshoot gadgets, and getting recruited for the most first rate activity you may ever ask for.

Following are the important ways and strategies thru which you could bring in coins.

Develop Your Mailing List

Everybody realizes that the coins is in the rundown, whether you are selling your personal objects and administrations or advertising accomplice gadgets. Here are a few extraordinary methods you could fabricate your mailing list on LinkedIn.

Make a LinkedIn bunch around an interesting and relevant concern. You can e mail new gathering individuals utilizing a custom invite format once they be a part of and one time every week. Develop your mailing by utilising welcome and declaration messages to strengthen free glad giveaways, on-line courses, and automated assistant instructive successions to get your collecting people on your rundown.

On the off danger which you can't exchange over people from your LinkedIn accumulating to your mailing list, clearly make certain to duplicate the main electronic mail you ship off your rundown each week (if pertinent) and glue it into per week after week statement e mail to your collecting.

Add your loose giveaway (digital e-book, record, white paper, and so forth) to the distributions segment of your LinkedIn profile. Individuals will simply want to navigate straightforwardly in your crush page. This is a fairly new area, and no longer piece of the not unusual association. You'll see it in the proper sidebar underneath "Suggested for you" while you go to your LinkedIn profile and tap the Edit button.

Try not to be enticed to add your LinkedIn contacts to your mailing listing. LinkedIn doesn't offer the choice to send out your contacts' records so you can upload them without agree to your mailing listing.

Sell Info Products

In the event that you are showcasing your own records item, LinkedIn can be an notable spot to get it accomplished. Here are far to utilize LinkedIn to get individuals into your deals pipe and onto your offers page.

Make a free piece of content. Free preparation recordings, white papers, reports, and virtual books are a simple method for buying possibly clients into your offers pipe. Share a connection to your weigh down page with your LinkedIn institutions and gatherings.

Welcome people to an online path. Online courses promising unfastened, important education (irrespective of whether or not individuals understand an attempt to close the deal is coming toward the cease) are likewise simple to raise in your LinkedIn associations and gatherings.

Offer LinkedIn limits. Individuals love saving. Make an terrific proposition code for your new object and offer it with your LinkedIn institutions and gatherings.

Add your new item underneath the ventures part of your LinkedIn profile. The ventures and distributions a part of your LinkedIn profile are the ones especially that provide the capacity to connection on your website online straightforwardly.

Exploit the advancement a part of gatherings you have a place with whose individuals would be ideal purchasers of your data object.

Find and companion with compelling people from LinkedIn to your area of expertise to check whether or not they could want to compose a survey or emerge as a member of your statistics item. Search for individuals with bunches of supports and recommendations as they may likely be people others gaze upward to and agree with for exhortation.

Know approximately comparative statistics gadgets that offer a non-public structures management bunch on LinkedIn for people? Observe that LinkedIn bunch. Regardless of whether you can't go together with, you'll see a rundown of the individuals which can be for your agency. Reach them to test whether or not they may be keen to your statistics item.

Sell Physical or Digital Products

Does your enterprise sell physical or automated gadgets? Here are a ways to utilize LinkedIn to amplify your offers.

Exploit the items a part of your LinkedIn agency page. Make man or woman object postings for your organization web page and absolutely use highlights, for instance, standards guests can snap to visit your presentation pages, sorts that focus on explicit sorts of customers, a YouTube enterprise or explainer video, and individuals to touch to discover additional.

Urge individuals to compose an offer on your object via adding the prescribe button in your object page. This will add social verification in your items when people find them for your agency web page.

Add a show, enterprise, or explainer video as a media component on your LinkedIn profile's define phase. Ensure that your media has a strong source of proposal and connection.

Engage in conversations inner bunches whose individuals are likely going to buy your object. Answer to posts brazenly or solution secretly when a response should activate a deal. In the occasion which you are a beneficial person from the collection, it's going to now not experience like a deal pitch.

StartupsPlus.Com This web site has wonderful monetize sources. They offer Premiun area of interest Premade Turnkey Shopify store with content material for Only $49.Ninety nine. These shops do have absolutely eye catching Premiun layout. The issues have already loaded up with merchandise on the market You can customize the fabric or maybe add more products to the shops. The high-quality component with Startups Plus is you acquire the grasp resell rights to resell the web site. That's wonderful concept to promote on LinkedIn.

This is the time to installation your business with out much effort. In this age of era, you want to apply modern methods to settle your commercial enterprise. For this reason, you need to release innovative websites to make your presence assured online. Moreover, some useful business courses are vital to walking your business. You can get all these items on-line on StartupsPlus.Com. The site makes a speciality of promoting premade web sites with content and PLR company commercial enterprise training substances.

Why do you need Pre-made web sites and education cloth?

As a new enterprise owner or a brand new weblog owner, you realize that your clients like to examine approximately the adventures and wonderful places or many others. In the e-trade enterprise, you are not the only one. There are numerous others online, and that they come up with a right away competition. If you want to stand out and be particular to enhance your purchasers, you want to use appealing and responsive templates on your on line commercial enterprise. This collection of 100% responsive web sites, innovative e-books, and other schooling cloth for on line users is an fantastic answer in case you need to refresh your e-commerce internet site. You will discover it easy to set up and implement. It is the excellent small enterprise opportunity for the majority of the human beings.

You will locate it notable as it contains a customizable, Homepage with equipped sections which includes custom content, testimonial, map, Single, product, featured product, slide show, brand list, image with textual content overlay, Gallery, image tabs, collection list, and blog articles.

It presents extraordinary integrated layout alternatives. This e-trade layout makes it less complicated to expand a expert tour website. You will locate special effects when you hover over the photographs. For footers and headers, there are numerous alternatives.

About StartupsPlus.Com

They promote websites and eBooks. If you want to get the first-class passive earnings commercial enterprise, you may order a internet site of other substances you can use on their commercial enterprise. The internet site can be used as a turnkey business. All you have to do is to promote the web sites that it sells. If you are new to the industry, you could customise this prepared-made fabric in your wishes, which includes internet site and eBook guides. Not most effective web sites, but you can also get other training material here that allow you to make your commercial enterprise a success. Learn greater approximately the features of the web sites which might be to be had right here on your assistance.

Innovative templates

The pre-made websites are designed with revolutionary templates. It carries several supportive answers for your on line internet task. Newsletter subscription shape, commenting system, social alternatives, and on-line chat offer a extra customizing experience at the web page. This topic consists of Megamenu and a set header. The retina-geared up template is ideal due to the lazy load effect; parallax scrolling is covered. You can use a solid MegaMenu or encompass an vehicle forex switcher to keep time for the customers. It enables the customers to organize the entire content speedy due to the drag and drop options.

High-first-class and relevant themes

This topic includes templates that present all styles of tours. Grab most capacity clients with pleased and shiny colorings with lovely bridge images, green mountains, seascapes, and palm bushes. It is a retina-geared up template with excessive decision. This subject gives easy navigation thru internet site pages because of the sidebar menu, tabs within the content material place, and visible banners. Above the product images, the welcome message is positioned. You can discover custom blocks under product photographs. It provided a rich collection of your sliders and hosted e-trade layout.

The cell-friendly subject matter facilitates users adapt web sites to mobile devices and the huge variety of screen extensions. The brilliant internet site gives a real-time verbal exchange with customers. Your clients do now not need to wait for a long term to fix their issues. It allows them to go through files to discover the solution to the problems.

a hundred% Responsive web sites

The pre-made internet site is ideal to seize the traffic for your website as it offers information on your clients about your products and services. For example, in case you want to settle your tourism enterprise online, the pre-made website can help your clients. They can get statistics approximately the traveler's destinations overseas, different critical details, prices, lodging, transportation, and many extra. You can take hold of the eye of ability clients and raise the site visitors' hobby by means of showing the pictures of the stunning sceneries inside the featured sections, sliders, and headers. Because of the aggregate of the attractive colorations, it gives a groovy look to your website online. Yellow is the dominant hue of this template that making it amazing.

It consists of an e-commerce design template that is exceptional for advertising purposes. By using this template, you may increase the search price of your website online. It is simple to optimize the website at the seek engine for an search engine optimization. This e-commerce template is available with online chat that establishes verbal exchange between you and your clients.

SEO-Friendly Website

The SEO-pleasant pre-made travel internet site offers an excellent choose for tour operators, tour tours, groups, and many others. Due to its absolutely responsive nature, you may be able to engage along with your customers. If you pick this astounding e-commerce layout with attractive pictures to your web pages, there may be no want to learn the code. The content hierarchy of the subject is easy and easy to recognize. This template is proper to provide 24/7 technical assist that is freed from charge, as well as it's miles richly documented. It gives e-commerce layout, attains hi-restock images and images totally free-lifestyles time use, and offers a web Chatbot and mobile-pleasant interface. It permits you to transport together with your initiatives on line. For offering the entire capability of the precise layout, this is an ideal subject matter in your journey business enterprise.

High-Quality pics

The splendid images and visual outcomes are the prime capabilities that make subject matters healthy to present a traveling provide. These templates are suitable for traders because they entice viewers due to splendid eCommerce designs. Amazing sceneries will compel them to have a pleasing holiday. The topics are excellent because of the easy animation with HTML plus JS. It lets in a cutting-edge look in your travel on-line keep website.

Offer Services

Independent newshounds, virtual amusement advisors, and different expert co-ops can utilize LinkedIn to accomplice with groups who want them inside the accompanying ways.

Streamline your LinkedIn profile to be found by means of those desiring to enlist you. Add your important watchword (SEO advisor, unbiased essayist, and so forth) in your profile's identify textual content, modern-day and beyond work titles, synopsis, abilities, and extraordinary areas. This will construct the possibility of someone locating you in LinkedIn listing objects.

Add abilities in your LinkedIn profile. This is the manner individuals give you rapid helps, and you additionally get the possibility of performing on a LinkedIn competencies web page. Many individuals determine to make use of administrations like Woorke to purchase Linked in Followers in the event that you want more genuine associations.

Exploit the administrations section of your LinkedIn organization page. Make postings for each certainly one of your administrations and absolutely use each of the factors like preferred images that connect to your web site, kinds of your administration portrayal that target specific forms of clients, video tributes, and individuals to touch to find out additional.

Characterize your most desirable patron (industry, top class, and so on) and join bunches they might participate in, as an example, land bunches for those wanting to develop their land advertising administration. Being gifted and supportive can prompt paintings requests, and having a similar gathering implies that individuals can message you with out a advanced participation.

If you would as an alternative now not accept as true with that capability clients will message you, message them when they ask the proper lead-in inquiries. On the off risk which you make Facebook pages, and any individual requests that how make a Facebook web page, answer their inquiry for certain essential advances openly and solution secretly to inform them you additionally provide this as an assistance.

Join bunches without cost specialist companies. These aren't your on the spot rivals, yet rather folks who might require your help every every now and then. For example, SEOs could require visible creators to make infographics for them. Independent journalists should require editors to go over their maximum current e-book. Network with these individuals within the amassing and you will be on their radar for the following time they or their clients need assistance.

Increment Book Sales

Do you have Kindle books on Amazon or virtual books for your own web site available to be bought? Here are some exclusive ways you may utilize LinkedIn to support offers.

Tell your contacts while you distribute some other book. You can ship customized messages to each one of your contacts (recommended) or ship personal messages to as much as 50 contacts unexpectedly. Add a task to satisfy with you to your message to build the possibility for individuals to expound on you and your new book on their weblog.

Add books and virtual books to the "Distributions" a part of your LinkedIn profile. The greatest aspect - you can do not forget a connection to books for Amazon or digital books for your web site so people can navigate to buy.

Join bunches relevant to the problem of the e book. Screen conversations for the precise open door to specify your e-book. To keep again from seeming as although a spammer, remember utilising the answer secretly choice to really let folks who pose inquiries in the gathering related with the book approximately it.

Make a video trailer to your e book. Add that video to YouTube and later on upload it as a media thing for your LinkedIn profile's synopsis place.

Compose a brilliant put up on your blog approximately your e book. Make certain to feature the LinkedIn proportion button to that blog access and later on proportion it together with your LinkedIn institutions in a note. On the off threat that your publish gets a ton of LinkedIn stocks, permit the LinkedIn enterprise development institution recognise so you get the opportunity of being highlighted on LinkedIn Today.

Characterize your book's ultimate crowd and make an commercial campaign toward LinkedIn clients that in shape that definition.

Track down Direct Advertisers and Sponsors

Assuming you provide selling for your website online or sponsorship valuable open doors for employer activities, LinkedIn makes it simple to song down predicted applicants.

Watch out for commercials in the LinkedIn sidebar, footer, and unique regions at some point of the website online. These equivalent companies might also likewise be attempting to find classified ads on sites or ready to aid events for gifted crowds.

Utilize LinkedIn's pursuit web page to tune down expected promoters and backers. You can restriction the consequences by using industry, business enterprise length, region, and extraordinary measures.

Track down the ideal individuals to contact on the business enterprise web page with the aid of looking beneath Employees on LinkedIn. Assuming that it is a touch corporation, you may peruse to music down the correct aid. Any different manner, you might want to put sources into an high-quality document so that you can make use of the excessive degree hunt channels and In Mails.

Advance Affiliate Products

Assuming that you use subsidiary advertising and marketing to provide pay on the web and compose brilliant surveys, then, at that point, here are some extraordinary methods you can elevate the ones on LinkedIn to build your offshoot deals.

Share your member selling audit affords as replies on cloth inquiries inner gatherings. On the off danger that somebody requests that how select the proper WordPress difficulty, and you have a publish searching at modified top rate topics (with accomplice connections), this is an wonderful threat to proportion it. On the off chance that the gathering does not allow joins, answer to secretly bunch individuals.

Assuming you have got your own amassing, ensure to email them about new survey posts on your weblog and any specials that they will be eager on, for instance, restricted time gives, rebate codes, and new object dispatches.

Have no distributions brought for your repertoire? Utilize the distributions segment of your LinkedIn profile to connection to your most recent subsidiary item audit posts.

Paid Speaking Opportunities

One extra method for adapting your Personal Brand on LinkedIn is through paid talking open doorways. Whenever you make a LinkedIn profile and start fabricating your personal picture, you consequently lay down an awesome foundation for yourself as a consultant for your enterprise. Assuming you put up massive substance constantly, odds are excessive that you may get speakme open doorways.

Makers regularly can't assist thinking about what the maximum ideal way to study speakme gigs is and how to pitch event coordinators. Assuming you fabricate a stable individual emblem on LinkedIn, odds are excessive that people will connect, without you while not having to „pitch" your photo to any of them. That is the pressure of net-primarily based enjoyment.

LinkedIn's Search Engine Optimization

Scouts are bound to discover your profile assuming you have worked actually difficult advancing your profile. In the occasion which you are gotten some statistics about the importance of search engine optimization, you will be happy to cope with that. Web optimization is a time period used to portray how Google and other web indexes rank your website(s). LinkedIn, similar to Google and different internet search equipment, utilizes search engine optimization strategies. Whenever an enrollment professional type in some thing like "content material writer" while looking for a project, this is the method through which it works. Accordingly, just streamlined profiles for the time period might be proven first. LinkedIn might be a splendid spot to search for a mission assuming you have got a stable deal with of website development (search engine marketing). You can keep in mind it the interaction via which web search tools discover you.

Incorporate a connection on your saleable object or administration.

Making an object to promote on LinkedIn is one method for bringing in cash. Data objects, as an instance, how-to manuals for buying outcome of their picked enterprise, are being offered by means of sure humans for advantage. Data things are unimaginably beneficial, and they are pretty regularly superior, inferring that they're affordable to create. Likewise, assuming you promote superior items, make it as truthful as doable for people to buy your object by basically tapping for your LinkedIn profile interface.

Get Hired

Try now not to have your very own commercial enterprise yet? Don't sweat it. LinkedIn can help you with getting the maximum high-quality activity you may ever imagine so that you love what you do from all day. This is the way.

On the off chance which you're attempting to find a specific kind of paintings, tools your LinkedIn profile to intrigue managers hoping to rent. Truly intend to wow them in your define segment by discussing the strength, revel in, and outcomes you offer of actual fee for that position. Utilize the media additives to add checks, tributes, and other noteworthy substance.

Assuming you have got a ton of supports for abilities linked with the gig you want, pass that straightforwardly underneath your outline. This can be particularly within the occasion that you have especially little professional training, instruction, or recommendations.

Chapter 7: How To Make Money By Means Of Blogging On Linkedin

Consider an exquisite feature.

A reasonable, sturdy function that vows to deliver worth to the peruser considers for a lot as 60% of the general development of your blog entry on LinkedIn, as functions catch perusers' eye in an undeniably packed scene. Utilize the feature to direct your substance, and bring the whole thing you would agree for your fine client.

For example, assuming you are a bookkeeper, you could strive "five Essential Tax Saving Tips This Year." If you are a private business enterprise improvement professional, you can strive "The Secret to Growing Your Business." If you're a spotter, strive "How to Find the Best Talent." Don't strain over offering your privileged insights!

Find or take a resounding photo.

The "legend photograph" straightforwardly beneath the feature counts for round 30% of the general final results of your post on LinkedIn, as individuals word images notably more than they notice textual content. A picture of you, otherwise you with another person that the publish will reference, is awesome. Picking and authorizing a image from a website, for instance, Shutter stock is some other choice. Never skirt the photo.

Compose a succinct post.

It is predicated upon what you want to carry, but frequently, four hundred-600 words is awesome. Utilize striking, italics, variety and rectangular statements to change up your publish. Consider implanting Slide share introductions or doubtlessly recordings through LinkedIn's not hard to-make use of toolbar.

Include two in range "guidelines to take action" on the decrease part of your submit.

Close your publish with two guidelines to do so for perusers: The first have to request that perusers observation and deliver them express inquiries to deal with related with your post. As remarks are a giant motive force of virality on LinkedIn, you may need to request comments out of your institutions and perusers. The 2nd supply of idea is a deal - this is the region where you'll power leads, promote books, or request software downloads. Drive individuals to a presentation page for your website with a supply of thought, as an example, "To discover extra, click on here." Consider an interactive image right here as nicely.

Share the publish on LinkedIn, Facebook and Twitter.

LinkedIn is maximum clear enterprise to share your submit on, for clear motives.

Consider sharing it both overtly (with your institutions as a whole) and secretly (through messages to key institutions). Consider presenting it to LinkedIn bunches you are in, and your enterprise page assuming you have got one. Go beforehand and proportion it as much as a couple of instances, as your partners and associates are signed in at numerous times at some point of that time and week. Request that your organisation percentage your submit with their organization.

Repeat tiers 1 through five.

To gather the quality consequences, weblog reliably, some thing like one time each week, on LinkedIn. Keep in mind, you don't have to contact one million people on LinkedIn to herald coins, you certainly need to arrive at a couple of the suitable individuals. Furthermore, chances are, irrespective of what you do, the correct people are in your LinkedIn corporation and your's organisation

How to make money Using StartupsPlus.Com LinkedIn

A representative is someone who plays administrations for an rate, whether or not this is hourly, consistent with phrase, or in line with project. At the cease of the day, specialists exchange time for coins.

With north of 680 million clients from one side of the planet to the opposite, there is a risk to bring in coins as a consultant on LinkedIn free of fee. LinkedIn gives you a more giant weather to interface with individuals to share posts and articles.

LinkedIn has additionally been appraised as number #1 level almost about Job search. This allows you as a consultant the possibility to analyze greater. A many individuals on LinkedIn are attempting to find associations they could paintings with.

You will determine out how experts can utilize LinkedIn to tune down unbiased paintings, how to look at greater rewarding customers making use of LinkedIn seek methods, and how to remain pertinent to your business enterprise in this online enjoyment stage.

You need to utilize LinkedIn each day to peer what your preceding editors ultimately rely upon now, to find out about the information you have to be aware of with contemporary clients, and as a element of your prospecting sports to track down new clients throughout everyday showcasing endeavors. Boosting your endeavors on LinkedIn is one of the abilties you ought to use to maintain a six-figure impartial enterprise.

Here are the some distinctive methods you can carry in cash on LinkedIn as a consultant;

Pick a Niche on Startups Plus

In the event which you're new to outsourcing, you may sense prepared to take ANY paid work you could get hold of. In any case, as you get in addition into your outsourcing profession, you'll have to start being extra key approximately the forms of paintings you do and the customers you're taking on.

We have already mentioned StartupsPlus.Com. We gonna dig little bit extra about this website. They sell Premiun Websites with content material. You may sell these web sites to nearly everyone on linkedin specially to the ones entrepreneur. They additionally selling one hundred thirty+ agency business training publications with PLR rights which mean you can placed your corporation call and brand and also allow to personalize the route materials. On LinkedIn there are alots of organizations of all sizes. You handiest need to discover the ones clients like the general managers, human assets managers, director or CEO. Every enterprise needs personnel trainings. Add these human beings normal and promote them the corporate enterprise schooling guides in a while. It can be perfect match!

Here you should be supposed for what distinctiveness you want to enter. Whether Graphic plan, Website configuration, Copy composing, Digital promoting, App improvement and so on..

In any case, you actually need to get an knowledge in the above specialties referenced. Getting the ones impartial know-how is quite simple this days with the help of YouTube and different academic exercising tiers.

Make a Good LinkedIn Profile Page

You actually need to make a respectable LinkedIn profile with each one in all your capabilities expressed. A profile web page draw in more clients or customers. Before any individual gets in touch with you for a assist, the character in question to begin with go through your LinkedIn profile to see whether or not you are the ideal decision to make it appear.

You can look in order that experts on LinkedIn may want to see version on how they approach having an appealing profile. This will widen your mind on the most talented technique to do yours as well.

Filter your institutions for refreshes. Skim your agency to check whether any person modified positions that could activate a probable client. You may want to leave a statement that is extra custom designed than handiest a 'like' or 'properly completed!' It's one of the sensible approaches of making use of LinkedIn to increase your unbiased enterprise. You should make notice of the touch's call, new company, and inside the event that they've a weblog on your pitching bookkeeping sheet to circle lower back to them in half a month within the occasion that they need impartial authors.

Look for online positions in a specific unbiased forte. For example, you could kind in "relaxation essayist" in the pinnacle hunt subject and afterward take a look at out "Positions" to look which businesses are recruiting complete-time positions in this strong point. This will deliver your mind of businesses to contact later for capability impartial composing function. Here and there you can send an electronic mail to an advertising and marketing manager at that second to check whether they need prompt impartial assistance whilst they may be hoping to fill that process.

Track down people to ship bloodless messages to. You can make use of LinkedIn to have a look at the names of promoting directors at organizations you're exploring to send an email prologue to. You may want to contact interface on LinkedIn assuming their e-mail returns and ship them a line or approximately what you do as an impartial substance showcasing essayist to test whether they want author.

Follow companies. This is one of the suggestions you can impart to training customers as an instrument to do not forget something person about the corporation for their virus e-mail pitch. Following organizations you want to paintings with on LinkedIn can let you know as to whether or not they've sent off new objects and have energizing declarations to percentage. This is one greater independent thriller of a way to get initiatives from LinkedIn.

Underwrite previous partners and customers for abilities. This may be a primary approach to attempt at the same time as utilizing the LinkedIn software to observe unbiased clients and you may have a couple greater of moments - like at the same time as trusting that supper will prepare. It assists that association with similarly developing their LinkedIn profile and it is a way that you stay pinnacle of brain with associations.

Compose posts and articles. To music down independent customers on LinkedIn and get independent undertakings from LinkedIn, you really need to amplify the corporation you worked there. I endorse sharing some thing mainly exciting you're chipping away at so capacity clients see this in their feed. I'll both proportion a connection to a new weblog entry and ask a next inquiry, or, I'll compose a completely unique weblog entry on LinkedIn.

See 'who saw your profile.' This is a decent method for seeing who is been assessing your LinkedIn profile and responsible it so as to join at the off risk that you trust it is somebody you could keen on work with. Go ahead and give them a message saying which you noticed they checked out your profile and you had to ask about any glad necessities you could assist with. You can utilize this approach to secure new independent composing positions, specially when independent it's far behind schedule to compose work.

Ensure your profile is present day. Whenever you turn in work for another client, you have to add that enterprise's name to my profile. You want to ensure which you are refreshing your capabilities, feature, and enjoy so that you are bound to seem in indexed lists when clients are attempting to find these competencies. Whenever you will add another impartial composing on the web route, upload it on your LinkedIn profile. Having a solid LinkedIn profile as a consultant can assist you with status apart on LinkedIn.

Chapter 8: Marketing Via Networking

Whether you're a new or set up commercial enterprise, certainly one of your modern-day biggest demanding situations is winning new clients and getting your message out to present customers.

Building a patron base requires advertising that frequently falls at the bottom of the priority listing for new marketers. But it's essential to don't forget that the use of the power of networking can generate extra leads than going it alone, because creating partnerships with other small businesses whose clients overlap together with your centered market however aren't your direct competition can boom the customer base for both partners.

So advises Gordon Deal of the Wall Street Journal on Small Business.

Mr. Deal states:

"Example of advertising and marketing via networking is when one associate is a social media organization and some other partner is the proprietor of a pc-repair business and their settlement is such that if any of social media employer's clients' point out having pc hassle, they might be recommended to call that partner. Likewise, if any of the partner's customers imply that they use social media for advertising, the companion will recommend the social media company for aid in that region." We can call it networking, however it's a basic community.

Networking, when it's accomplished right, is extensively conventional as the one of the most cost effective and worthwhile strategies for generating new commercial enterprise.

The concept of community marketing isn't new. Often it entails phrase of mouth. For example, if a person recommends a brand new restaurant to friends and acquaintances, who then in flip inform others about it, the network effect is at work. A well-known character may be capable of create a big network of believers round a given product. For example, a TV celebrity recommends a book to his or her viewers and suddenly it will become a hit.

Another explanation of networking is that humans regularly generally tend to talk to people like themselves; their shopping for tastes might be comparable regardless of whether or not they ever speak the product. Social principle tells us that folks who talk with each different are more likely to be just like each different, and this concept is referred to as homophily. So, related consumers possibly are like-minded, and like-minded purchasers generally tend to shop for the equal products.

Now, all of us realize that organizations are for all time searching out ways to become aware of and goal potential clients, and being capable of do it better could both store them money and boom income. Marketing campaigns are highly-priced and now not effective if the right human beings aren't targeted. Therefore marketers have long used all types of demographic and geographic statistics to target ability customers — their age, gender, training level, profits, put up code. But once more there's a price powerful variable that businesses can also need to don't forget: it is clearly who is connected to whom!

So, now, let's outline networking in a nutshell: Networking it is a business and private marketing tool in order to supply your standard commercial enterprise and advertising approach.

Networking architect Heather White says - In advertising terms, networking as a tool, will display you in which to find destiny enterprise possibilities instead of immediate effects. But established networkers do acquire immediately results, which is why all enterprise people must be or emerge as exact at networking.

Networking is particularly properly-applicable to any business focused on consultative selling, account-based totally advertising, and referral advertising in addition to localised markets. It additionally works tremendously properly if you are looking to interrupt into new markets, learn about your competition, deepen your knowledge approximately your customers and other kinds of market studies.

It is a private shape of verbal exchange and normally involves face-to-face contact so then networking deepens your enterprise's connections.

People nonetheless purchase from people first. If human beings are to shop for from you due to the fact they believe you, you need to be nicely related and feature a credible profile in your market.

Ok, we've got it! Networking works! But what are your networking alternatives?

With restricted time and assets to spend on networking, it is probably tempting to assume you may do it all on line in recent times. But assembly commercial enterprise contacts face-to-face at networking occasions, conferences and exhibitions is still essential to build agree with and develop leads.

Founder of advertising consultancy Kintish Limited, Will Kintish, who is a leading professional in networking inside the UK says "You can start business relationships on-line, but it's only while humans study your frame language, smile and shake arms that they really want to do commercial enterprise with you".

So, begin through finding out what sort of networking alternatives are beneficial on your commercial enterprise zone. These may be offline or online and don't need to be honest networking occasions.

Will Kintish stresses: "Too many human beings don't engage with different delegates at a conference, and spend all their time at an exhibition with the aid of their own stand". Any platform or occasion in which commercial enterprise proprietors get collectively is a networking opportunity for you. And you shouldn't miss that. Check nearby business guide enterprises or chamber of commerce events calendar for upcoming activities on a steady foundation.

2.Online vs Offline Networking

Now let's evaluate on-line as opposed to conventional networking alternatives

Penny Power, founder of commercial enterprise networking website online Sunzu (formerly called Ecademy), says: "The key gain of on-line networking is convenience: it can take location at any time and you do no longer need to tour for networking. It additionally exposes you to a much broader pool of capability contacts who you can pinpoint in a manner that eliminates the risk that characterises many conventional networking events".

She keeps "By being lively you could construct your community quite fast. Aim to make the maximum of every contact you get. Remember, in case your touch can't help you at once, they might refer you on."

But, consistent with Mr. Kintish you must now not forget about physical networking options too, because they're a good way to construct an enduring relationship. Networking on line is a 'virtual handshake', no longer a alternative for face-to-face networking.

Things from time to time work a whole lot quicker if you meet someone, and it's less difficult to assess if you need to do commercial enterprise with each different. Before identifying which platform or activities to goal, you need to have a clear concept of what you want to get out of them.

Think about your objective, finances and how much time you need to spend. For instance, your objective is probably to locate new clients for your target market or suppliers in a specific enterprise.

So, make time to make the most networking options

There are lots of networking businesses, and it may be difficult to decide which the exceptional ones are to spend a while on. Make the most of any slow durations, via building up your touch base. If you don't have a great deal work on, it may be useful to attend two or three networking activities in step with week and find new clients this way.

Always make time to go to occasional networking activities, perhaps out of doors of your regular operating hours. You can sign on with platforms like meetup.Com and internations.Org to find you next networking event!

Next logical query is:

When does networking take place?

Word-of-mouth advertising is occurring irrespective of what. People are always speakme about different people.

Jeff Bezos, the CEO of Amazon, says, "A emblem is what human beings say approximately you while you aren't within the room". I might add: "That is how networking takes place". It is the espresso chat, the water-cooler verbal exchange. Here's an instance on how one such goes:

Person A says: "How's that project going?"

Person B replies: "Not too awful, but Mark has dropped out, so we've got come to a grinding halt!"

Person A: "Have you found a substitute yet?"

Person B: "No, we're struggling to find someone we are able to believe and who has the proper competencies."

Person A: "I know simply the proper individual..."

The act of turning up, enticing with humans, leaving a exceptional affect and staying in contact will give you those future enterprise opportunities. And in case you do not construct the ones relationships, a person else will.

3. How to Use Networking for Lead Generation

So, you already have a community, now, how to use it for lead technology?

As in keeping with Will Kintish, the UKs main advertising and marketing professional, in a small or medium-sized enterprise or a expert partnership there should in no way be a need for bloodless calling. You can generate leads within your network. Stop for a moment and remember what number of human beings you understand. It will run into masses, for instance, your:

- Existing customers
- Other professional contacts
- Friends
- Family
- People on the sports activities or social membership
- Committee contributors you can paintings with

These corporations are the gas that would be used to generate leads and propel groups into the huge time. Pool your assets with all of the other key people to your workplace and you've got were given a big and treasured database to begin with.

See each invitation that lands in your table as an opportunity for lead generation. Grow your current community. So when you see the subsequent invitation, say to your self: 'Aha, that is a chance for me to fulfill new contacts, to make new sales or boom my costs!'

While on the occasion work the room. If you experience a chunk shy and fearful to network and to speak during the occasions, don't worry. Most humans at networking occasions sense exactly the identical and handiest the most carried out and everyday networker will feel relaxed.

But what's the real problem? Why do we experience anxious to technique someone? For maximum people it's miles worry of rejection. But the famous international motivational speaker Zig Ziglar says: 'Fear? Its a...False Evidence Appearing Real!'

Do you remember, how regularly have you been rejected at a business or occasion? When was the last time a person turned their returned on you, not noted you or rejected your extended hand? Kintish states 'no matter how frequently I ask those questions from marketers, the answer is usually NEVER'.

So take a deep breath, method a person new, introduce yourself and ask for his or her name. They will mentally hug you for coming near them as they're probable greater fearful than you.

Networking is like gaining knowledge of to drive or getting to know to touch-kind - it's usually a bit uncomfortable before everything. But how long does this feeling ultimate? You'll soon sense simply as comfortable approximately networking as you do behind the wheel of your automobile or at your laptop.

Remember, you don't necessarily usually need enterprise from the humans you're approaching, however you can ask them the question: 'Who do you realize who may be interested in...As an instance, your carrier...?'. People, typically, want that will help you with lead era. Why? Because it makes them sense desirable! They are assisting the community!

So, work the room enthusiastically, your confidence will construct, you may start to experience these occasions and new commercial enterprise will flow.

There's a common subject matter to using, typing and networking. Practice and a fantastic mind-set make ideal. Ask your self 4 questions:

• Am I excellent at what I do?

• Do I provide a extremely good service?

• Have I were given the ability to take on more?

• Do I want more costs or income?

If you can answer 'yes' to some of these questions, then go away your workplace, and start looking! If you doubt your self, then perhaps you better enhance your tender abilties.

Like I noted in advance the idea of networking fills some human beings with fear whilst others think they may be wonderful at working a room. But what are the abilties you want to be a great networker? And how will you enhance your performance? Heather White of Smarter Networking has the answers.

She says: To be a a hit networker, you want to have enormously advanced soft capabilities, or inter-non-public abilties, in addition to a strategic attitude. Assessing your own abilities may be hard. But it enables to apprehend your very own strengths and weaknesses before you try to improve your networking capabilities.

Here is the list of the tender competencies you want a good way to community effectively. What I want you to do is score your self on how well you think you do on every the front.

Before you examine yourself, permit me also point out that you must now not take each of the subsequent statements to extremes, because the overriding talent is to act appropriately in the scenario you locate yourself in. Download the following desk at the lowest of this lesson and rating yourself among 1 (low) to 10 (excessive).

See the table beneath:

Soft talent Self rating - between 1 (low) and 10 (excessive)

I am honest

I am decent and revered

I am an energetic listener

I am an awesome conversationalist

I am an influencer

I am confident

I am a negotiator

I am a problem solver

I'm willing to engage

I'm inclined to proportion

I can read others and respond therefore

I am a very good observer

I am properly at such as others

I can keep confidences

Where you have got scored yourself low, you now realize what you need to paintings on to enhance your networking performance. If you've got rated your self particularly, pass and check this out with your contacts to ensure you are studying the scenario correctly. If the whole lot stacks up, do greater of what's running.

four. Building Trust and Rapport

Next issue you need to understand is to build consider and rapport.

People purchase from humans they prefer and believe first. In impact, they're shopping for consider, professionalism, expertise and like-mindedness.

Remember the golden policies of networking: being likeable, constructing consider and rapport, planting seeds approximately your expertise:

• Build the communique, basing it on not unusual ground.

- Show true curiosity.

- Learn a way to read body language.

- Listen and find out how the particular person you're speakme to prefers to talk.

- Stay engaged at some point of the conversation.

- Develop the conversation.

- Become the observer of others; be aware their technique to things, and take this into attention.

- Work for your human beings abilties and treat others as they would need to be handled.

- And then...question and concentrate

- Ask more questions, in preference to just talking approximately your self.

- Talk approximately what you do only if invited. Don't pressure your statistics on others.

People most effective concentrate whilst they are prepared to, so create that opportunity. If someone else is speaking, allow them to end their point. Make sure you pay attention them out definitely, and do completely have interaction. After all, in case you do not hear them out, why might they want to listen to you?

It is OK for a verbal exchange to complete without you having contributed information approximately your self.

Memorise at least ten correct time-honored questions, remembering that excellent questions assist to stimulate the verbal exchange.

Be proper and fresh every time you ask a query - even when you have asked this a thousand instances over.

Listen carefully and body your next question out of the response.

Be cautious now not to make the method sound like an inquisition.

Your face, voice, eyes and body language have to explicit real interest, not a found out approach.

Heather White also recommends: If you notice the 'glazed look', take inventory of what you're talking about with regards to the character concerned. Very quick convey the communique to a prevent and ask a query to re-engage them. To boom the strength again, you could use humour and even a few cheekiness!

Sometimes, the glazed look is certainly due to the fact the other person is considering what you have stated, so you can allow silences (extreme human beings do that a lot!).

If you agree with this man or woman is not involved, thank them for their time and allow them to pass on.

All conversations have a natural rise and fall, so has a while arise? If so do not dangle onto them.

The biggest tip I can offer you is while you are subsequent at a networking occasion stand again for some time and just watch humans. Watch for how humans reply to others and spot who's getting it incorrect and notice folks who are becoming it proper. Listening and staring at can be the exceptional manner to research.

Here are some inquiries to get the conversations flowing recommended via Allison Graham who's a company trainer and keynote speaker specializing in powerful networking. So the primary query is:

"What's your connection to the occasion?" This query while asked in networking events can find mutual contacts and generally leads to an improved solution than if you requested the typical "Have you been to this event earlier than?"

"What's retaining you busy while you're not at activities like this or at work?" This question gives the encouragement vital for the individual to share his/her passions and outdoor pursuits. It is an extremely good way to feature some enthusiasm right into a verbal exchange that has hit a lull, particularly if he/she might favor to be doing that interest at that moment.

"Are you getting away this summer time?" This question can cause conversations about own family, display unique interests and, if you like speakme approximately travel, it's a sure-hearth way to hold a verbal exchange exciting.

"Are you working on any charity initiatives?" This question makes it smooth to release into a deeper connection. If they're no longer involved with any projects, they frequently percentage reasons that is commonly revealing, and if they are doing something of fee they will be more than happy to share.

"How did you become in your line of work?" For some, the course to wherein they're nowadays may be pretty an exciting ordeal. Having a hazard to revisit their story to success can leave beneficial clues along the manner as to who they may be and what makes them tick.

Keeping a communique rolling is simple when you discover ways to concentrate and ask appropriate probing questions that certainly grow from the speak. You best need to put together a couple of questions in advance. If there is a proper connection then you can proactively have interaction in conversation.

Do not forget about on-line networking due to the fact you community offline. Simultaneously with offline networking you could run campaigns on line or possibly outsource it on your crew. But attempt to be present on line and offline at the same time.

five. How to Use Online Networking for Marketing

Now, I am going to give you the approaches that you may use social networks to marketplace your business enterprise and yourself, write them down if you may. The first tip to grow to be successful with on-line networks is:

Researching your market. Listen greater than you communicate is prime in gaining knowledge of. Through participation in community discussions, corporations can study patron pastimes and reactions with a candor not often observed in consciousness corporations and surveys.

Create Competence. If becoming an expert for your subject is a part of your advertising and marketing method, social networks come up with a far more accessible outlet than the media. You can speak up in a mailing listing, dialogue discussion board, or weblog, and attain hundreds or lots of human beings. Say some thing useful, authentic, and profound, and you'll get quoted and linked to, attaining even extra human beings.

Build and enhance your brand. Every signature in an electronic mail or at the Web, and every profile on line, is an possibility to enhance your logo. Link to your groups out of your Web site. Link on your private profile page out of your community web page. Link, link, link.

Unveil a human voice. Networked markets demand openness from the organizations who need to sell into the ones markets. Organizations should have extra human beings participating in reality than simply expert entrepreneurs. A satisfied employee is a more effective brand evangelist than nearly all people in Marketing. This is one cause why Microsoft has approximately 1,200 bloggers out of fifty five,000 personnel.

Associate your self with a now not-for-income motive. People are lots extra inclined to acquire round a cause than a corporation. You can create a network round a reason or topic associated with your emblem. Music companies, movies, authors, and plenty of technology agencies can regularly guide a community around their emblem. However, many different organizations do now not have that sort of user base. Instead they can build a network round a reason, as Avon does with its Breast Cancer Crusade take a look at out for reference: www.Avonfoundation.Org/breast-most cancers-campaign.

Microtarget. If you have identified a selected narrowly-described companies to goal, the percentages are right that you can identify a digital network where they may be already collected. Are you promoting consulting services to impartial bookstores? If it would not already exist, just create a digital community for your target pool, seed it with your closest relationships, and watch it grow.

Ignite phrase-of-mouth buzz. If you have got a brand new services or products, word-of-mouth—happy clients speaking approximately you—is one of the handiest approaches to set up your Competence. Word-of-mouth flows through social networks; Leaders of networks are outstanding lighthouse customers. If the most distinguished blogger on your area likes what you promote, you may create a powerful evangelist.

Remember, there is a not unusual mistake many entrepreneurs make when coping with online communique, it's in wondering that it may be turned on and rancid like an advertising marketing campaign. Online networks are typically now not very receptive to advertising messages from trendy members. You need to earn the proper to speak about your product via participation in and contribution to the community. Similarly, you can't really depart when the campaign is over, or you may be visible as shallow and a "user." People do not need to be used; so please do not use humans.

6. Action Steps to Take

Once you've got hooked up your non-public presence and commenced developing your community on-line, here are steps you could take to leverage virtual relationships for advertising:

Pull, don't push. Focus on awareness, not persuasion. Your participation, your signatures, and your profiles will create recognition. Those who're fascinated could be interested in you and could come to you for greater records and help.

Create a widespread template for e mail and Web signatures for all of your personnel. Reinforce your logo with each verbal exchange. It can be simple text, however it's clean enough to comprise your organization logo, as well. However, some humans do now not consider intricate signatures suitable for trendy correspondence.

Be constant, now not persistent. Long gaps to your participation will be noticed, and in case your participation simply peaks for the 2 weeks earlier than your advertising marketing campaign, humans will see it as manipulative.

One of the high-quality networking platforms on line which you have to be thinking about is Linkedin. LinkedIn is the largest professional community for operating humans. It doesn't remember if you're an employee or a enterprise proprietor, a freelancer or a marketer inside a organization.

We endorse you to have a relationship mentality when on LinkedIn and to put yourself as a notion leader. Look where you're building influence along with your network and niche. It's the proper aspect to do when it comes to attracting leads and people to your enterprise. The smarter you're approximately marketing, the much less people recognise you are advertising and marketing to them.

Your main intention is to goal to be consistently seen and precious.

So, it's truely vital to keep your LinkedIn profile updated. The more people see you on LinkedIn, the more they're possibly to return and take a look at out your profile to research extra about you. And if that individual is applicable and potentially interested by your business, they may click thru on your weblog or internet site and take the connection from there.

Consider Linkedin Groups for networking. If you spend time in institution discussions, you've got the possibility to connect to mutual institution members whom you might not always know. As you get to know some of the individuals inside the group, you could ship them an invitation to connect to you.

If your goal is to generate business and leads on LinkedIn, you want to think about developing your connections. There are many exceptional approaches to connect, from meeting human beings offline to connecting with them on Facebook or Twitter. Think about friends in your enterprise, customers, prospective customers, network leaders, and so forth.—every person you may realize and have an excellent motive to be connected with.

LinkedIn has a characteristic called InMail. Open charges for InMail on LinkedIn are extra than open costs for common electronic mail advertising collateral. InMail offers you the ability to send an instantaneous message to any member of LinkedIn, no matter whether you are connected to them. The response rates on those are excessive.

But do not forget, you've got to have an excellent motive to connect, online or offline. It can't be just a sales pitch of your services or products. It is higher you discover companions via networking to team up and promote every different's merchandise to their very own network. Teaming up with humans who have strengths in which you have weaknesses is constantly a wise approach in networking.

7. Practical Advice on How to Start Networking Successfully

Time came for practical advices. In this chapter you will find practical advice on the way to start networking successfully, those tips have been shared via contributors of marketingdonut.Co.United kingdom, a domain in which you discover greater assets for small groups to set advertising goals and plan advertising approach and mix. Check out marketingdonut.Co.United kingdom for extra information.

So, permit's get began. First factor first, don't just attend any event, attend events organized, researched, therefore the first advice is:

Research networking events

First issue is first: List your key commercial enterprise wishes.

Your commercial enterprise dreams, any difficulties you might be experiencing and areas you need to improve should manual your wondering. Try to expect the wishes you may have in the future.

Your listing might include attracting funding, finding a enterprise companion, sourcing a new supplier, beginning up new markets and increasing your expertise or abilties.

Networking with human beings from similar backgrounds who face similar challenges helps you to percentage thoughts, help every other and develop confidence.

Think about who should help you to fulfil those wishes.

Next for your wishes, listing the varieties of human beings, companies or corporations that might be capable of provide answers.

Develop a general idea of each. Where are they located? What can they offer you with? What will they count on from you?

Identify businesses they're related to.

These will be professional bodies, exchange associations, boards or interest businesses.

Find other companies that are relevant to you, your business, zone, location or unique interest. To do that, study the exchange press, enterprise directories or seek online. Seek statistics out of your local business help business enterprise or Chamber of Commerce. Also ask your financial institution manager, legal professional and accountant, in addition to your providers and customers.

Think approximately the possibilities provided by means of your current social networks. For instance, community groups and neighborhood commercial enterprise people you recognize. Consider getting greater worried.

Check whether your competitors belong to a trade affiliation, expert frame or community.

Find out approximately applicable networking occasions.

Add the contact information of all applicable establishments for your information. Important web addresses should be added in your favourites and visited frequently.

Discover what offerings they provide, who their individuals are and what events they stage (for instance conferences, seminars, mentoring or training programmes and social gatherings).

Discover while, in which and why such events take place. If you cannot discover enough statistics online, contact companies without delay. Ask whether or not you have to be a member to wait their activities. If so, discover about membership charges and benefits. If activities are open to non-members, discover whether you need to pay to wait. You can locate applicable activities on-line via Google and Meetup.Com, Internations.Org or Eventbrite.Com.

Get organised

Schedule networking events to your diary. Rearrange other appointments earlier if these war. Don't cancel them because these offer networking opportunities, too.

Base your choices upon your business priorities.

Differentiate among the significance of activities.

Guided by using how tons time you can spare and how in all likelihood you're to reap worthwhile objectives, comprehend which events you need to attend and which ones are less essential.

Don't goal to attend all occasions. If you cannot attend an vital one, make sure someone else is there to represent you if feasible. Networking must be the duty of all agency representatives - not simply the owner-manager.

Formulate a 20-2nd presentation about your commercial enterprise.

You could be able to use this while you meet humans at networking activities.

This have to encompass:

Continually reconsider your strengths, USP(s), value and needs. You need to ensure that the things you say approximately your commercial enterprise are updated while you meet humans at occasions.

Your key commercial enterprise strengths and specific promoting proposition (USP) - those differentiate you out of your competitors.

Information about what value your business can provide. It is not enough to actually talk about what you have got furnished to your clients - you want to bring what it enabled them to gain.

Recent crucial information about your corporation (as an example prevailing a new agreement or investing in new equipment).

Your key commercial enterprise needs.

Prepare for an event

Get a list of attendees in advance if feasible.

Arm yourself with information about essential human beings and their business enterprise or business enterprise. These are the people you discover as being maximum possibly to fulfill your key business wishes. Names and job titles are generally listed alongside company names in events literature. Learn more by way of journeying their websites.

Create a shortlist of humans you want to fulfill. Know what you want to invite them and put together your self for any questions they might ask you.

www.ingramcontent.com/pod-product-compliance
Lightning Source LLC
Chambersburg PA
CBHW071220210326
41597CB00016B/1890